Dennis R. Maynard

The Sweet Smell of Magnolia

WWW.EPISKOPOLS.COM
Books for Clergy and the People They Serve

To order additional copies, please contact us.
BookSurge
www.booksurge.com
1-866-308-6235
orders@booksurge.com

DEDICATION

This book is dedicated to you, dear reader.

Without you the story would have ended with Book One.

COVER DESIGN

I am grateful to Chris Koonce of Fort Worth, Texas for designing the cover to this book. He is a very talented young artist. Chris earned a Bachelor of Fines Arts degree in 1991 from the University of North Texas. I encourage you to visit his website to view his portfolio of artwork. There are several opportunities for personalized gifts for yourself and others. He can also be a resource for fundraising opportunities for your organization, parish or school. Please visit his website at:

www.kcfunart.com

BOOKS BY

DENNIS R. MAYNARD

THOSE EPISKOPOLS

This very popular book serves as a great introduction to the Episcopal Church. It also reaffirms the love for this Church that so many loyal members have for her. Well over 100,000 copies have been read. It has been called "the unofficial handbook" of the Episcopal Church. Clergy in virtually every diocese in the American Church use it in their new member ministries. It seeks to answer the questions most often asked about the Episcopal Church. Questions like: "Can You Get Saved in the Episcopal Church?" "Why Do Episcopalians Reject Biblical Fundamentalism?" "Does God Like All That Ritual?" "Are There Any Episcopalians in Heaven?" And others.

FORGIVEN, HEALED AND RESTORED

This book is devoted to making a distinction between forgiving those who have injured us and making the decision to reconcile with them or restore them to their former place in our lives.

THE MONEY BOOK

The primary goal of this book is to present some practical teachings on money and Christian Stewardship. It also encourages the reader not to confuse their self-worth with their net worth.

FORGIVE AND GET YOUR LIFE BACK

This book teaches the forgiveness process to the reader. It's a popular resource for clergy and counselors to use to do forgiveness training. In this book, a clear distinction is made between forgiving, reconciling, and restoring the penitent person to their former position in our lives.

THE MAGNOLIA SERIES

BEHIND THE MAGNOLIA TREE (BOOK ONE)

Meet The Reverend Steele Austin. He is a young Episcopal priest who receives an unlikely call to one of the most prestigious congregations in the Southern United States. Soon his idealism conflicts with the secrets of sex, greed, and power at historic First Church. His efforts to minister to those living with AIDS and HIV bring him face to face with members of the Klu Klux Klan. Then one of the leading members of his congregation seeks his assistance in coming to terms with the double life he's been living. The ongoing ministry of conflict with the bigotry and prejudice that are in the historic fabric of the community turn this book into a real page-turner.

WHEN THE MAGNOLIA BLOOMS (BOOK TWO)

In this the second book in the Magnolia Series, Steele Austin finds himself in the middle of a murder investigation. In the process, the infidelity of one of his closest priest friends is uncovered. When he brings an African American priest on the staff, those antagonistic to his ministry find even more creative methods to rid themselves of the young idealist. Then a most interesting turn of events changes the African priest's standing in the parish. A young associate undermines the Rector by preaching a gospel of hate, alienating most of the women in the congregation and all the gay and lesbian members. The book closes with a cliffhanger that will leave the reader wanting another visit to Falls City, Georgia.

PRUNING THE MAGNOLIA (BOOK THREE)

Steele Austin's vulnerability increases even further when he uncovers a scandal that will shake First Church to its very foundation. In order to expose the criminal, he must first prove his own innocence. This will require him to challenge his very own Bishop. The sexual sins of the wives of one of the parish leaders present a most unlikely pastoral opportunity for the Rector. In the face of the ongoing attacks of his antagonists, Steele Austin is given the opportunity to leave First Church for a thriving parish in Texas.

THE PINK MAGNOLIA (BOOK FOUR)

The Rector's efforts to meet the needs of gay teenagers that have been rejected by their own families cast a dark cloud over First Church. A pastoral crisis with a former antagonist transforms their relationship into one of friendship. The Vestry agrees to allow the Rector to sell the church owned house and purchase his own, but not all in the congregation approve. The reader is given yet another view of church politics. The book ends with the most suspense filled cliffhanger yet.

THE SWEET SMELL OF MAGNOLIA (BOOK FIVE)

The fifth book in the Magnolia Series follows the Rector's struggle with trust and betrayal in his own marriage. His suspicions about his wife take a heavy toll on his health and his ministry. He brings a woman priest on the staff in face of the congregation's objections to doing so. Some reject her ministry totally. Then the internal politics of the Church are exposed even further with the election of a Bishop. Those with their own agenda manipulate the election itself. Just when you think the tactics of those opposed to the ministry of Steele Austin can't go any lower, they do.

All of Doctor Maynard's books can be viewed and ordered on his website WWW.EPISKOPOLS.COM

BOOKS FOR CLERGY AND THE PEOPLE THEY SERVE

FORWARD

When I'm invited to be a guest preacher or speaker around the nation, I am often approached by a priest or lay person with a story. They are anxious to share their story with me. The stories in these novels are the catalyst that motivates them to reveal their own experience. Some of the stories are humorous while others are filled with pain. Many of the storytellers have walked in the shoes of Steele Austin. They've lived in toxic parishes and been targeted by the dysfunctional members of the congregation. The smallest infraction or error in judgment is embellished and magnified to portray the priest as a dark and devious person better suited for the penitentiary than the ministry. Too often these *clergy killers* honestly believe that they have been divinely called to remove the priest from their parish. In many cases, they try to try to end the priest's ministry completely. Always they excuse their reprehensible behavior by saying that they are doing what is best for the parish.

While the stories in these novels are fictional, they are not unique to the people of First Church. One of the reality lessons about the contemporary Church is that far too many clergy and lay leaders have all had the experience of doing combat with wolves wearing sheep's clothing. Clergy routinely work fifty and sixty hour weeks. Couple that with the intense caring that connects them to the lives of the people they pastor and the combination makes them even more vulnerable to stress related diseases. The end result of being attacked by the very people they are trying to serve has left multiple clergy, their spouses, and their children suffering with Post Traumatic Stress Syndrome. Even if they find another parish and exercise a faithful ministry, their sleep will be interrupted with flashbacks and night terrors for the rest of their lives. They end up seeking long term psychiatric care that includes prescription medicines for depression, anxiety and sleep deprivation. Many often end up living with debilitating and life threatening diseases that clearly are the product of the trauma they experienced in their parish.

The real sadness for many of the faithful lay people who were supportive of their priest but caught up in the parish power play is equally tragic. Most often they walk away from the Church, never to return. This only adds to the pain of the afflicted priest. Toxic parishes that have been traumatized by a power struggle with their priest often enter a period of decline in giving, attendance and membership. Few recover and it often takes decades for the ones that do to find renewal and begin to grow again.

Clergy enter the ministry to bring people into the Church and to nurture their spiritual lives. I think it's safe to say that parish conflicts like those personified in the stories of The Reverend Steele Austin have never brought a single soul to Christ or to a sojourn in the life of his spiritual body on earth.

The truth of the Gospel and the ministry of the Church are not minimized by these encounters. The great miracle of God's grace is seen in the wonderful ministries that are manifested in spite of the small group in most every congregational system that works to derail them. The Gospel Story remains the greatest story that can ever be told. These evidences remain and transcend the silly parochial conflicts that cannot be minimized.

My youngest son, Andrew, had been in the restaurant business for several years. For a brief period he worked with me in a parish. One day he became particularly exasperated with a couple of demanding members. He said to me, "Dad, you put up with behavior in this parish that would get those people thrown out of a decent restaurant."

The Church welcomes all. Every conceivable personality type is welcomed. Those who are ill in body, mind and spirit are welcomed with open arms. Jesus reminds us that the healthy do not need a physician. Those who know their sins all too well will find the doors of the Church standing wide open for them. But the welcoming arms of the Church are also extended to those who believe they are without sin and all too willing to cast the first stone. This is the Church of Jesus Christ. It is made up of imperfect people. The good folks at First

Church in Falls City, Georgia mirror most every congregation in the world. God continues to use imperfect people to accomplish His purposes on earth because no others are available.

In these novels I've attempted to put a human face on the very issues that the people in our world live with on a daily basis. As a result, they are the very issues that too often get politicized in the Church. In every congregation there are men and women who feel trapped, even shamed, into living a double life, thus hiding their sexuality. Women are the Church's most faithful members, but too often they are treated as second-class citizens. Priests are not immune to having married foolishly or impulsively. Likewise, they can find themselves trapped in loveless marriages. Too often, they seek less than honorable solutions to their loneliness. Racism is not dead. Poverty is still with us. And Church leaders too often find themselves more concerned about being in control than being faithful stewards of the Church's resources.

If the characters in these novels do, in fact, paint a human face on these and other manifestations of the disease that we all share by virtue of our common humanity, then I've achieved my purpose. My hope from the beginning was that these novels would not just be a source for individual reading, but that they would stimulate discussion in book clubs, Sunday school classes, staff and Vestry meetings.

On the following pages I've listed the names of the primary characters in these stories. I've also included the reasons that I chose to name the various personalities as I did. You will see that I've borrowed from scripture, television, music and literature. It will also give you a further insight into the perplex ways my mind operates. For this I apologize, but as my oldest son, Dennis, continually reminds me — *it is what it is.*

Several of the characters themselves continue the lives of those revealed in scripture. The ministry of Simon Peter, Zacheus, Mary and Martha, the woman caught in adultery, Lazarus, Jairus' daughter, and others. I leave it to you, dear reader, to read and re-read the books in this series, keeping the Gospel story in mind. You will find multiple parallels.

My hope from the beginning has been that my readers would be able to see the several Biblical similarities as the story line unfolds.

The people at First Church live out the Biblical story. There is sickness and healing. Love and forgiveness walk hand in hand. Hopelessness is overcome by miracle. Evil is ever present but God still accomplishes his purposes. And the reality of death is always faced with the hope and promise of the resurrection.

My heartfelt thanks to each of you for your words of encouragement at my book signings, and in your thoughtful e-mails, notes and letters. You are the reason that the lives of the people in Falls City continue to unfold. My special thanks to you for sharing my work with those in your community. Thanks for encouraging your local bookstores to stock my books. And my special thanks for talking about my books to the people you know. There is no higher compliment an author can seek than a satisfied reader that recommends their work to others. You are my best advertisement.

Faithfully,
Dennis R. Maynard, D. Min.
Rancho Mirage, California

THE PRIMARY CHARACTERS

The Reverend Steele Austin
Rector of First Church (Episcopal).

I chose to call him *Steele* because of my own childhood fascination with the *Man of Steel, Superman* that I watched fly across my black and white television screen every Saturday morning. I chose *Austin* for his last name out of my unending affection for The Republic of Texas.

Randi Austin
Wife of Steele Austin and mother of his two children.

Randi is actually short for Miranda. The name means *wolf shield*. Randi is Steele's source of healing, renewal and protection. In William Shakespeare's play, *The Tempest*, Miranda is the daughter of Prospero. One of her most memorable lines is "I might call him a thing divine." Such is her love and devotion to Steele. I chose to call their son Travis as a further tip of my hat to Texas. Their daughter's name choice is intensely personal and will receive no further explanation.

Almeda Alexander Drummond
Self- appointed matriarch of First Church.

I wrestled at length to try to find the perfect name for this particular character. It finally came to me when I overheard a teenager remark to her dad, "It is all about me, duh!" Hence I came up with the contraction, Al- me-da.

Chadsworth Purcell Alexander
Steele's invisible but ever present guardian.

My first inclination was to simply name this character *Chad*. In an earlier portion of my life I enjoyed listening to a rock ballad by Kay Hanley. The ballad includes the words *I just want a life. I don't want to hurt anyone, but sometimes you have to."* The refrain is *Chad saves the day.* I believed it descriptive of this character's double life and his continuing role as the one that rescues Steele and his ministry. Since *Chad* seemed too adolescent, I chose to expand it to *Chadsworth*.

Earl Lafitte
Chadsworth's longtime secret gay lover.

Earl is a name that means warrior and brave man. His name is given to mark the courage it took for him to claim his identity as a gay person. Lafitte was a gentleman pirate, but in this case I chose Lafitte because Club Lafitte is reportedly the oldest gay bar in America. It is located in New Orleans.

Rufus Peterson
The Bishop of The Diocese of Savannah.

Ayalah Friedman wrote one of my favorite children's books. The primary character is a rooster by the name of *Rufus*. He declares himself to be the king of the chicken yard. I felt the name *Rufus* could best describe this character's arrogant approach to his Episcopate.

Stone Clemons
Parish Chancellor that pledged his loyalty and support to Steele.

I had Jesus' apostle and staunch defender Peter in mind when I chose the name of this character. *Peter* or *Petros,* meaning *the rock.* I chose to name him *Stone,* echoing *Peter, the rock* in Jesus' life. Does this character not also remind you of one of my favorite humorists, Samuel Clemons? Stone echoes much of the common sense wisdom of Mark Twain.

Chief Sparks
Chief of Police and insightful advisor to Steele.

This character is known simply as *The Chief.* While it is not his first name, it is descriptive of the role he plays in the book. In the tradition of Native Americans, the title *Chief* meant wise man or sage.

Henry and Virginia Mudd
The model couple from an aristocratic Falls City family.

Henry is a name applied to the head of the house. Virginia finds its origin with Elizabeth the First, the virgin and virtuous Queen of

England. The Virginia in these novels is neither. Mudd is symbolic of the scandalous life Virginia chose to lead, splattering plenty of mud on all that crossed her path, including her husband and children.

Delilah Cummings
Henry Mudd's new love.

Delilah is from the story of Sampson and Delilah, but only in this case instead of taking away the heroes' strength, she heals his broken heart.

Rob and Melanie McBride
Friends of Steele and Randi. Godparents to their daughter.

Rob is a synonym for stolen. Rob is representative of the several priests that I've known in my life that literally had their ministry sabotaged through no fault of their own. Melanie brought a new song into his life. In my first draft she was named Melody.

Horace Drummond
Steele's Senior Assistant, and second husband to Almeda.

I had in mind the first century freedman and poet, *Horace,* for this character. His last name *Drummond* I recalled from a novel I read as a teen about a freed slave by the same name.

Howard Dexter
Steele's early antagonist and Senior Warden.

The role of this character can be found in the synonyms for the word *dexter or dexterity*—on the right, conservative, shrewd and cunning. He plays the role of the *Keeper of the Treasury* in the parish.

Willie and Grace
The faithful sexton at First Church and his wife.

Willie and Grace go together. They are two faithful people in the Lord's service. I chose the name Grace for his wife because she portrays the very essence of that divine gift.

Josiah and Rubidoux Williams
Steele's good friend and his wife that pastor the African American Parish.

Josiah means *the Lord saves*. A great name, I thought, for this servant of God. I chose Rubidoux as the name for his wife simply because I liked it. It is also the name of one of my neighboring communities here in Southern California. I thought it accurately described this colorful character.

Ned Boone
Steele's constant and unrelenting antagonist.

I had no intention of confusing this character with Daniel Boone. My intention was to describe him physically as a *jester*. His role, while extremely antagonistic, could best be viewed objectively as that of a buffoon. Hence his name.

Martha Dexter and Mary Alice Smythe
Faithful workers, but self-appointed defenders of the tradition.

These names have an obvious origin. I had in mind the faithful companions to Jesus, Mary and Martha.

Elmer and Judith Idle
Relentless adversaries of Steele Austin.

The sin of idolatry is recognized as an extreme devotion or admiration of a false god. The god of Elmer and Judith Idle bears little resemblance to the God of love, compassion and forgiveness revealed by Jesus and preached by Steele Austin. The name *Idle* finds its origin in *idolatry*.

Gary Hendricks and Tom Barnhardt
Leaders determined to separate the parish school from parish control.

The name Gary Hendricks finds its origin in the words *spear and ruler*. The words *twin, strong and bear* evolve into the name of Tom Barnhardt. I wanted to give these two characters names of warriors determined to do whatever was necessary to get their way.

"Dear Heaven, I give thee thanks...
Because I can still see
the bloom on the white magnolia tree!"
Helen Deutsch

BOOK FIVE

Chapter 1

VIRGINIA MUDD WAS stoned. She had passed out on Alicia Thompson's couch. Alicia had been Virginia's confidante and shield the past few years. She had used Alicia to cover for her with her husband Henry when she was having an affair with Jacque. Alicia had allowed Jacque and Virginia to use her lake house for their weekly rendezvous. She had also allowed them to use her home for their trysts. Now that Virginia's adulterous affair had become public knowledge in Falls City, Alicia was about the only friend that Virginia had left.

Drool slithered out of Virginia's open mouth onto the couch. The combination of marijuana, alcohol, and sleeping pills had given her the escape she needed. In a blackened state her dream world had carried her back to a happier time in her life. She was the toast of the social elite in Falls City. Her volunteer life brought her much attention and many accolades. She was quite frequently pictured on the society pages of the Falls City newspaper. Her lifestyle was envied by all the women in the city, with the exception of those who occasionally shared the spotlight with her.

She had the perfect life. She had married a wealthy attorney from an old and distinguished Georgia family. She had two beautiful and talented daughters. She lived in a big house on River Street. She had been born to wealth and privilege. She loved the lifestyle that came with being Mrs. Henry Mudd. At First Church she was highly regarded and received the respect and deference afforded a lady in her position.

An involuntary smile crossed Virginia's face as her dream world opened into her dining room. She was busily making sure that her long time servant, Shady, had everything in readiness for the family breakfast. Shady and Virginia were the same age. They had even played together as children. But Shady was her cook, housekeeper, and nanny to Henry and Virginia's two daughters. Virginia was actually very fond of Shady, but now Shady was her *help*. The relationship between the employer and the *help* was clearly defined by custom. And custom had to be honored. Their relationship could be cordial, but Shady needed to be reminded from time to time as to just who was employer and who was servant.

Lost in her dream, Virginia was happy. She saw her two daughters enter and embrace her. They were so beautiful and carefree. They were both excellent students at First Church Episcopal School. They were popular with their friends. Virginia was so proud of them. They took their places at the table. Henry came into her dream and kissed her on the cheek. He smiled a broad smile at her and then kissed each of his daughters on the tops of their heads. Virginia walked over to the dining room buffet to see if Shady had remembered to fill the silver biscuit box. Then she felt Shady grab her arm. Shady was shaking her arm and shouting at her, "Virginia…Virginia…"

"Let go of me, Shady. Stop it! Stop that, I said. Go get the biscuits…" Virginia opened her eyes to a blur. It was Alicia. She was shaking her arm.

"Virginia, wake up. Just look at this mess you've made. There are empty glasses and dirty plates all over my house. Look at yourself, Virginia. When's the last time you took a bath? Virginia, I hate to tell you this, but you smell."

Virginia struggled to sit up on the couch. She rubbed at her eyes. "What? What are you talking about? Why did you wake me? I was having the best dream. I was home with Henry and the girls. We were preparing to have breakfast. Everyone was so happy. It was just wonderful. I didn't want to wake up."

"Get a grip, Virginia. Those days are over and they're never going to return." Alicia was busily picking up the dirty dishes and carrying them to the kitchen. She returned with a trash container and started tossing the empty potato chip bags, candy wrappers, and frozen food cartons that Virginia had left on the floor into it. Clearly, Alicia was angry. As she emptied the ashtrays she glared at Virginia. "Just how many joints did you smoke today? My God, Virginia, you've turned into a lush. Do you have any idea just how fat you've gotten?"

Virginia started to cry. "I thought you were my friend."

Alicia stopped and looked down at Virginia. "Face it, girl. I'm the only friend you've got left in this town."

"Well, friends don't talk to their friends that way."

"No, Virginia, you're wrong. You asked me to be the kind of friend that tells you what you need to hear and not what you want to hear, and that's exactly what I'm going to do."

"Well, you don't have to be so mean about it."

Alicia carried the trash container to the kitchen. When she returned, Virginia had once again stretched out on the couch and closed her eyes. "Sit up, Virginia. It's time for us to have a serious talk."

Virginia twisted her body so that she could sit up. She leaned her head back against the couch. "God, my head hurts. I feel so drowsy. I just need to go back to sleep."

"No, Virginia, what you need is to start taking care of yourself. You need to make a plan and get on with the rest of your life."

"What life?" She whined. "My husband has thrown me out of the house. My girls won't talk to me. Everyone in Falls City knows what I've done. Don't you get it, Alicia? I'm the town whore. I have *a big red A* pinned to my chest. I don't have a life. Just what am I supposed to do now?"

"I honestly don't know." Alicia sat down on the sofa chair across from Virginia. She lit a cigarette and stared at her friend for several minutes. At one time Virginia had been a beautiful woman. She used to have an attractive figure, clear complexion, and radiant eyes. She was the image of the pampered society wife in her designer clothes and manicured nails. Now she was stretching out the seams on the muumuu she was wearing. Virginia waddled over to the liquor cabinet and poured herself a glass of scotch. She returned to the couch. Alicia knew she should feel sorry for her, but she didn't. Virginia had no one to blame but herself. Most any woman in Falls City would have traded places and gladly assumed the role of Mrs. Henry Mudd. Virginia had risked it all for an adulterous affair with a handsome face. Virginia had destroyed her own life and in the process almost destroyed Alicia's as well.

Virginia whimpered, "Don't you think if I give Henry just a few more weeks, he'll stop being so angry with me and I'll be able to go back home?"

Alicia sat back in her chair and let the laughter pour out of her. "Oh, for God's sake, Virginia. Have you lied to yourself for so long that you've lost touch with the real world? Henry is never going to take you back and he's going to make you pay for the pain you've caused him and your daughters. Hell, Virginia, have you forgotten that he tried to make me pay for your adultery as well?"

A look of confusion washed over Virginia's face. "You? You... Alicia? How has Henry tried to make you pay?"

"I'll swear, Virginia, I think all the pot, booze and pills you've been swallowing have taken their toll on your brain. Have you forgotten that the police raided my house two weeks ago looking for drugs? They were planted here, Virginia. If my neighbor hadn't been looking out his window and saw those guys climb into my bedroom window while I was at work, I'd be in the county jail right now. He noticed that they had backpacks on when they came in, but they didn't have them when they left. He figured rightly that they had left something here. I had hardly gotten home, found those backpacks and taken them to his house to hide when the police arrived. Who do you think had those drugs smuggled into my house?"

Virginia gave Alicia a blank stare and then started shaking her head. "Oh, I don't think Henry would have done anything like that."

"Wise up, Virginia. Henry found out that I'd been covering for you and Jacque and he wanted to get even with me. No one else in this town has a motive to try to hurt me but him. And I wouldn't be a bit surprised if he didn't try something again."

Virginia swallowed the last of her glass of scotch and then stood to go refill her glass yet one more time.

"Sit down, Virginia!" Alicia shouted.

Virginia collapsed back onto the sofa. "You scared me, Alicia. Why are you yelling at me?"

Alicia lit another cigarette and took a long hard look at her friend. "Virginia, this just isn't working."

"What's not working?"

"You staying here with me. It's time that you find your own place and get on with your life."

"With what, Alicia? Henry has taken my checking account away from me and he's not giving me any money. What am I supposed to do? Where am I supposed to live?"

"It's time you get a lawyer. My hunch is that you're going to need one anyway. Get it through your head, Virginia. Henry's not going to let you move back in with him. I want you to get an attorney first thing tomorrow morning. As soon as he's gotten you a living allowance from Henry, I want you to move out."

Just then Alicia's doorbell rang. A young man greeted her and asked for Virginia Mudd. Alicia called Virginia to the door. "Are you Mrs. Virginia Mudd?

"Yes."

Mrs. Henry Mudd?"

"Yes."

"I have a package for you." The man handed Virginia a padded envelope.

"Who's it from?" Alicia asked as she closed her door.

"It doesn't say."

Virginia opened the package. She pulled out a videotape and turned it over so she could read the label. The blood drained from Virginia's face. She felt like she was going to faint. She began to sink as Alicia grabbed her and helped her back to the couch. Alicia took the tape from Virginia. She read the label...*Naughty Housewives Uncovered.*

Chapter 2

THE RIGHT REVEREND Rufus Petersen, the Bishop of Savannah, was relaxed but exhausted. He had allowed himself the one indulgence that some of the more proper members of his Diocese just might consider inappropriate. Once a week for the past thirty years he had driven to the outskirts of Savannah. He knew the route by heart. He didn't even have to look for the number of the farm to market road. He would pull up in front of the white house with bright blue trim and go around to the side door. Once inside, he would take off all his clothes, lie down on the table, and wait for one of the young women to join him. Then for the next ninety minutes he would allow her to massage his naked body from head to toe.

Rufus had never been able to attract a woman. He was not tall in stature and had been cursed with a huge appetite. The inevitable consequence of that combination was a body that was just about as wide as he was tall. After his heart attacks last year he had lost a lot of weight, but now his skin hung loosely on his skeletal frame. The contents had been removed, but he was left with the empty envelope. At least for a while each week, he could close his eyes and enjoy the gentle touch of a beautiful woman.

Following his massage, one of the young women would bring him a soft robe and some slippers. She would take his hand and lead him to the solarium. Here she would seat him in a comfortable lounge chair next to a gentle waterfall. She would burn some incense and offer him a cup of hot tea to drink. He could remain in the solarium as long as he wanted. If he wanted more tea, he only needed to ring the little copper bell sitting on the table next to his chair.

Rufus sat staring into the pond beneath the waterfall. He watched the large Japanese carp swimming gracefully among the lily pads. Rufus was lost in his thoughts. He so missed his good friend Robert Hayes. Bob had been so much more than his Chancellor and advisor. Bob had been his best friend. Truth be told, Robert Hayes was his only friend. A shudder ran up his spine as he thought about the last task he had given his friend to do. Rufus had asked him to go to each of the priests that he felt like he'd betrayed as their Bishop. He so wanted to put things right with each of them. Robert Hayes had done as Rufus had asked, but to no avail. Every one of the priests that he visited on the Bishop's behalf had rejected the appeal to forgive and reconcile.

Rufus put his face in his hands. He tried to blot out the image of Robert Hayes putting a gun to his temple. His efforts were useless. Tears poured out of his eyes and into his hands. He wiped them on his robe and laid his head back against the chair. Rufus Petersen could not escape the fact that he had failed so many of the priests that had been given into his care to shepherd. He had fed them to wolves dressed in sheep's clothing. While Bob had told him that some of these clergy had overcome the trauma that brought their ministries to a conclusion, the lives of most were in ruin. Rufus knew it was his fault. For the past year, he'd had to live with the guilt that his best friend's suicide was his fault as well.

Rufus rang the little copper bell. A young woman with long red hair and a radiant smile entered the solarium. She was wearing short shorts with spiked heels. Her shirt was tied at her waist and opened just enough to expose her ample bosom. "Yes, Tom..." Rufus had told her that his name was Tom. "What can I do for you?"

Rufus forced a smile. "Darling, would you bring me some more of this hot tea? I wouldn't mind if you put a little brandy in it."

"Sure enough, Tom. I can do that." She put her hands on her hips and struck a pose that was unmistakable in its intent. "Are you sure there isn't something more I could do for you? I promise I'll be real gentle and you will have no regrets."

Rufus studied the vision standing so close to him. There was a time in another life when he would have given everything he had for the opportunity to possess her for even a few minutes. Then he shook his head. "You are a gorgeous woman. I'm sure that you have many suitors. I regret that I can't be one of them. I'm a tired old man that needs only to sit here for a while longer. I'll just take the tea and brandy, but thanks anyway."

Disappointment washed over the young woman's face. "Well, if you're sure. But if you change your mind, ring the bell."

Rufus nodded. "Just the tea and brandy for now."

Not only had the death of Robert Hayes left an empty place in Rufus' life, but it had also left him without an able assistant to help him with his ministry as Bishop. The doctors had told Rufus he needed to slow down, so he'd hired a Canon to the Ordinary. He now regretted that decision. Not the decision to employ the help he needed, but the person that he'd chosen.

Canon Jim Vernon had been a mistake in so many ways. Rufus knew that he'd been criticized for the choice by other Bishops, his own priests and lay leaders in his Diocese. Canon Vernon had never graduated from a theological school. His education had been through the Diocesan school that was really designed for the education of working Deacons who had no aspirations for ordination to the priesthood. He'd never served as the head of a congregation of any size. The Canon's only job had been as an office manager for a not-for-profit organization. He'd been fired from that position. The Bishop interviewed him to be his Canon soon after. He'd given him responsibility for overseeing the mission clergy in the Diocese and screening and recruiting new clergy. Jim Vernon assumed his new role with vigor.

It only took a few weeks for the Bishop to realize that Canon Vernon had his own agenda. He liked being in control and had little patience with anyone that didn't succumb to his demands. To disagree with him was to not love him. Clergy and lay leaders had started bringing their complaints about Canon Vernon to Rufus not long after he hired him. The Canon would only let search committees look at extremely conservative clergy. Many, like himself, were without degrees from Episcopal seminaries. Within months, the Canon had replaced several mission clergy in the Diocese with radically conservative clergy.

It was the Canon's ability to manipulate Rufus that had caused him the most grief. In order to get his own way with clergy and lay leaders, Jim Vernon was not above appealing to Rufus Petersen's lower nature. On more than one occasion, his Canon had withheld information, twisted the facts, and even fabricated things about a particular priest or lay leader. He had the ability to use these tools to work Rufus Petersen into a steaming rage. When it came time to confront the recalcitrant person, Rufus Petersen would be so angry as to be without reason. He found himself resorting to a behavior he had promised his departed mother he'd overcome. Rufus Petersen would enter a meeting room on the attack. He would be yelling at the top of his voice and making veiled threats demanding that the target of his anger conform to the Canon's instructions. The Canon, in the meantime, would simply sit in the corner trying to disguise his look of pleasure.

As he sat there next to the waterfall drinking his tea and brandy, Rufus knew that Canon Jim Vernon was manipulating him but he was just too tired to do anything about it. Rufus did not like the person that the Canon to the Ordinary was bringing out in him. He wanted to be a better person. He didn't want his clergy to fear him. He certainly didn't want them to despise him. After his heart attack, he was determined to be the kind of Bishop he felt God and his sainted mother wanted him to be. He realized that this new Canon was causing him to fail miserably.

Rufus closed his eyes. He tried to pray. Words failed him. He was empty. He felt so far from God. At one time, he'd really enjoyed being Bishop. He'd loved all the trappings. The cope, mitre, ring, and crozier had been objects of pride for him. He was pleased to be able to wear the purple shirt. He loved the deference and respect that was given to him simply because of his office. All the trappings of being a Bishop that had brought him so much satisfaction seemed downright silly now. They all seemed so empty and without merit.

He thought about the Episcopal visit he had made last Sunday. He dressed up in his cope and mitre to parade down the aisle of the little parish church. There were no more than forty people present. The little flock was so sincere in their devotion. They were excited to have their Bishop visit. The Rector did not have a single person to present for confirmation. In fact, there were no infants or young people in sight. The average age in that little parish had to be seventy. As they each presented themselves at the altar for communion, he felt like he was ministering to the walking dead. The ladies of the parish organized a picnic on the grounds following the Mass. Two elderly gentlemen cornered him. Their agenda was so familiar. They wanted to know just what he was going to do about the homosexuals. The National Church seemed to be out of control. They didn't want any of their contributions going to the Presiding Bishop. They'd heard rumors that they were going to revise the Prayer Book again. They were against it. And the litany continued for well over an hour before the Rector rescued him. It was the same thing at every visitation. The entire performance just seemed downright useless to him.

The hours that he worked in his office each day weren't all that different. At least once a week he received a visit from lay leaders unhappy with their priest. Invariably they wanted their priest removed. Their complaints ranged from sloth to rumors of sexual immorality. Then there were the priests who wanted to move to new congregations. They felt they'd done all they could do in their current assignment. They needed a bigger challenge with more responsibility, which Rufus translated into wanting more money.

Then there were the endless committee and board meetings. There was never enough money to meet the needs of the various organizations. The frustrations of the committee members ran deep. All looked to him to find the pot of gold that would solve all their problems. He knew that none existed.

Rufus took a sip of his tea. By now it was lukewarm. He drank it anyway. He was grateful the young woman had exaggerated the amount of brandy she put in the cup. He thought of the gatherings with his fellow Bishops. His Diocese was one of the smallest in the National Church. Consequently, he was at the bottom of the totem pole in the House of Bishops. The Bishops of the large Dioceses had the most money and inevitably the most power. Their voices carried more weight. His influence on the decisions of the House of Bishops was next to insignificant. Even in the House there were agendas and divisions. The conservative Bishops grouped together, but so did the liberal ones. He often felt that those wanting change were steamrolling their ideas over others like him that valued tradition. At his first meeting of the House of Bishops he remembered feeling so insecure. He thought he had truly risen beyond his level of competence. He wondered if he should even be a Bishop. Now, all these years later, he wondered the same thing about his fellow Bishops.

Once again he closed his eyes and reflected on all the expectations that came with the office of Bishop. They were so familiar yet so very exhausting. He just didn't care anymore. In the grand scheme of life he asked himself just what he had accomplished. He was tired. He was just too tired to fight anymore. Rufus tried once again to pray, but no words formed in his soul. He just sat there listening to the waterfall. Then, in the stillness, the answer he'd been searching for came to him. Rufus Petersen now knew exactly what he must do.

Chapter 3

"PLEASE, MISTURH AUSTIN. Please, please reconsider. Think about what you're doing to this parish." Mrs. Gordon Smythe pleaded. Mrs. Smythe had been president of the Altar Guild for as long as most members of the parish could remember. Very few in the First Church congregation could even remember the name of her predecessor. There was no heir apparent and no current member would dare challenge her for the position. She insisted on being addressed formally by her married name. Only her closest of friends could call her by her given name, Mary Alice. The Reverend Steele Austin had not been afforded that privilege.

"Listen to us, Misturh Austin. We know this parish better than you do. You simply must receive our counsel on this subject." Mrs. Howard Dexter was the other self-appointed keeper of the traditions at First Church. The two women had alternated between their opposition and support of Steele Austin's ministry at First Church. Without fail, they had organized an opposition force to every new idea he presented. Their army invariably was made up of the Altar Guild members. But without fail their opposition would dwindle to passive acceptance with the passing of time. In spite of their denials, he believed they had some level of devotion for him and his family.

"Ladies, I understand your concern. I want to thank you for making this appointment and bringing your reservations directly to me." The two women had requested the appointment with Steele. He really appreciated this change of behavior. Up to now their pattern had been to ambush him at a meeting of the Altar Guild or manipulate their husbands into doing so at a Vestry meeting. That had been his experience to date with those opposed to his ministry innovations in the parish. He was hoping that this signaled a new and healthier level of dialogue with the congregation.

"Misturh Austin, we know of that which we speak." Clearly, Mrs. Smythe was trying to control her anger. It appeared to Steele that she just might be on the verge of tears.

Mrs. Howard Dexter wasn't keeping her anger under control quite so well. Her face was bright red. The redness of her skin could have been easily hidden considering that a Cheyenne Indian readying himself for battle wore less war paint. Steele continued to wonder just why she would put so much rouge on her cheeks. Evidently she never blotted her lipstick, as it always looked freshly applied. Invariably she had lipstick on her two teeth that protruded over her bottom lip. "The women of this church will not tolerate a woman priest! Do you hear me, Misturh Austin! This is unacceptable!"

Mrs. Smythe reached over and patted her on the hand. "Now, now…we agreed that we would present our case in a civil manner. So please, let's all stay calm."

Steele watched the dynamics between the two women. Some time ago he had learned that while Mrs. Dexter had some very definite opinions, she always deferred to Mrs. Smythe. "Obviously, you both are women. Can you help me understand just why you would object to a woman priest?"

"It's just not seemly." Mrs. Smythe responded in a voice that was little more than a whisper.

"I beg your pardon."

"The priesthood is man's work."

"Do you know any women priests?"

The two women shook their heads. Mrs. Dexter couldn't contain her anger any longer. "No, and I'm not sure I want to. They're all lesbians anyway."

That response caught Steele off guard. "Why on earth would you assume that all women priests are lesbians?"

"Because my niece is one." Mrs. Dexter practically spit the words at Steele.

"I'm sorry. I thought you said that you didn't know any women priests."

Mrs. Dexter glared at him. "I haven't spoken to her in years. Her own father and mother broke off communications with her when she chose her deviant lifestyle. Now she calls herself a priest."

"Was she ordained in the Episcopal Church?"

"If that's what you want to call it."

"So you assume that all women clergy are lesbians since the one female priest you know is a lesbian. That's quite a reach."

Mrs. Dexter looked at Mrs. Smythe. "Mary Alice, I think we're wasting our time here. It's apparent the Rector has already made up his mind. He's going to do just what he always does. He's going to do it his way and what the rest of us think just doesn't matter."

"You may be right, but we agreed that we would come in here and present our case in a civil manner. He's agreed to listen, so let's not give up on him just yet."

Steele smiled. "I want to thank you for that. I realize that bringing a woman priest on the staff is a change that might take some getting used to. Remember, you both had reservations about Doctor Drummond."

Mrs. Smythe nodded. "Yes, and that's taken some getting used to. I don't have to tell you that not everyone in this congregation has accepted him. There are some who will never accept a black..."

Steele interrupted, "African American priest."

"Oh, whatever." Mrs. Dexter waved her hand at him. "I've worked at a relationship with him because he's married to one of my best friends. If Almeda hadn't married him, I would probably still be outspoken in my opposition."

"But you would agree that he has won the hearts of a great many people in this parish."

They both nodded.

"Then what makes you think that a woman priest wouldn't prove herself to be an asset to our parish?"

"I said that I had worked on a relationship with Doctor Drummond because he married Almeda. I'm not about to agree that he's an asset."

"Hardly." Mrs. Smythe agreed.

"Well, in time I hope you'll both come to realize that his ministry in this parish is quite valuable."

Neither woman responded. Then Mrs. Smythe broke the silence. "We didn't come here to talk about Doctor Drummond. We came here to voice our objections to hiring a woman priest."

"Okay, let's see what I can do to address some of your concerns."

Mrs. Smythe reached into her purse and brought out a small note pad. Steele noticed it was in a Gucci leather binder. "First, there are no other women priests in this Diocese, so how do you think that will sit with them?"

Steele shrugged. "I really don't know. I can tell you that I discussed it with Bishop Petersen. He agreed that it was time that a woman priest was brought into the Diocese, and he also agreed that First Church was the logical place to begin. "Why?" Mrs. Dexter's anger presented itself once again. "Why do we have to be first? We were the first to hire an African American, as you insist we call him. We were the first to start a Soup Kitchen. We were the first to...oh, forget it. Just forget it. I give up."

Steele leaned toward her. "Please don't give up. Please let me try to help you understand. I don't regret any of the good things we've done. All of them are ministries that Jesus has called us to do. I believe Jesus would want us to expand our ordained ministry to include women."

Mrs. Smythe smiled. "I'm so glad you brought Jesus into this discussion. If Jesus had wanted women priests, why didn't he call a woman to be one of his apostles?"

"Custom." Steele spoke in a calm voice. "In order to establish himself as a legitimate Rabbi, Jesus had to get twelve men to become his students. Any teacher that couldn't gather at least twelve men to follow them could not call themselves a Rabbi. Jesus worked within the customs of his time to establish his credentials. But remember, women played a major role in his ministry."

"Yes, Misturh Austin. I agree. Women shared in Jesus' ministry, but not as apostles." Mrs. Smythe was pleased with her response.

"Ladies, the Episcopal Church has studied this issue theologically and concluded that women can, in fact, be ordained as Bishops and priests. We have several thousand women clergy and several women Bishops in the church today."

"But not everyone recognizes them!" Mrs. Dexter shot.

"That's true. There are a handful of bishops, priests and lay people that still do not accept them. But the parishes that have opened themselves to the ministry of women clergy have found their lives blessed and their ministries enriched. I personally know many women clergy and I have been blessed by them and their gifts."

"That may be so." Mrs. Smythe appeared to be reflective. "Let's say that you do bring a woman priest to this parish. Just what are we supposed to call her — *Mother?*"

With that both women chuckled.

"You and other members of this parish have a difficult time calling me *Father.*"

"The Bible is clear on that one, Misturh Austin." Mrs. Dexter snorted.

Steele was amused. "Let's do a study on just what that passage means at another time. For right now, I can tell you it has nothing to do with how you address your priest."

Mrs. Dexter rolled her eyes at Mrs. Smythe. Steele smiled at both of them. "Addressing priests as *Father or Mother* is a custom that finds its origin in the religious life. It has to do with the titles given the heads of the monasteries and convents. But how we address her need not be an issue. If you are not comfortable calling her *Mother* then do as you do with me, call her by her first name or simply *Mrs.*"

"What does she look like?" Mrs. Dexter twisted uncomfortably in her seat.

Steele wasn't prepared for that question. "I think she's a very attractive woman. She has silver hair trimmed close to her face. She has crystal blue eyes. She's a runner, so she takes very good care of herself. She's quite slim. She's about my height."

Steele noticed that his answer had made Martha Dexter even more uncomfortable. "I think I have a publicity picture of her on my desk." He retrieved the picture and handed it to Martha.

Martha stared at the picture for a minute and then frowned, "You said we could call her *Mrs.* so I assume that means she has a husband?"

"No, she's divorced."

"Divorced!" Mrs. Dexter shouted as she rose to her feet. "I've heard enough. Let's go, Mary Alice, I'm going to call the Bishop and every member of the Vestry and block this nonsense. We're not going to have a divorced priest of any kind in this congregation. We're especially not having a divorced woman priest flirting with all our husbands. Why, it's no telling what she might do with one of our men once she gets them behind a closed door."

"And you'd draw that conclusion without even knowing her or her circumstances?" Steele continued to remain calm.

"I don't care about her circumstances." Martha Dexter stomped her stubby little foot on the floor. "I'll not have it! Do you hear me? I'll not tolerate it."

"Sit down, Martha!" Mrs. Smythe stated emphatically. She watched Martha Dexter sit back in her chair. "You have my attention, Misturh Austin. Tell us her circumstances."

"This is what I can tell you without breaking any confidences. The woman is the mother of two teenage daughters. She has been raising them by herself for the past ten years. Her husband is completely out of the picture and has not seen his daughters since he moved out a decade ago. I can also tell you that her husband is currently married to a woman twenty years his junior. Do you really need to know more?"

Both women sat in silence for several minutes. Mrs. Smythe broke the silence. "Have you already hired her?"

Steele nodded. Again, there was silence. This time it was Steele that broke the silence. "She'll begin her ministry here in one month."

The two women looked at each other. Simultaneously they stood. Mrs. Smythe extended her hand to Steele. "Misturh Austin, I just don't understand what there is in you that causes you to push this congregation to the limits. I just hope this doesn't end up being your swan song. I have to tell you that I fear that this might be the final straw. I pray to God that I'm wrong."

Mrs. Dexter was standing at the door to Steele's office. She opened it and looked back at Mrs. Smythe. "Let's go, Mary Alice. We've been wasting our time."

Steele walked over to Mrs. Dexter. "I'm really sorry that you feel that way. I consider you to be one of my friends. I value your opinion. I just want you to give Mrs. Graystone a chance."

"What's her first name?" Mrs. Smythe inquired.

"Ginnifer, spelled with a G."

Martha Dexter broke out in laughter. "Ginnifer Graystone – GG, sounds like a stripper's name. Oh, Misturh Austin, you've really gone and done it now."

The two women left his office. He watched them as they were walking down the hallway. He could still hear Mrs. Dexter laughing as they exited the building. Steele walked to his office window so he could look out at the steeple of First Church. Maybe this wasn't the best time to push the parish. He had other problems. He turned and opened his center desk drawer. He pulled out a large brown envelope. He had no need to open it. He'd memorized the contents. There were suggestive pictures of his wife and another man in the envelope. He'd been able to think of little else over the past couple of weeks. He still didn't know what he was going to do with the pictures. For the first time since he'd married Randi, he had doubts about her and about their marriage. He knew that he had to do something to resolve his suspicions and doubts, but what?

Chapter 4

HENRY MUDD WAS sitting in the back booth of Daisy's Café. Dee was snuggled up against him. He had his hand underneath the table and was stroking the top of her bare leg underneath her dress. She had removed her shoe and was rubbing his leg with her foot. The waitress at Daisy's had been observing both of them over the past few weeks and knew to give them lots of alone time when they came in for an early lunch. They always ordered the same things, so she would wait twenty minutes or so after pouring them coffee before bringing their meals. Dee always had the chef's salad with the dressing on the side. She seldom ate all of it. Henry would nibble at his chicken fried steak but seldom finished it either. They both did eat their *beat'n biscuits*. Evidently the woman had never eaten them before. Daisy had to explain to her that the thin little biscuits were called *beat'n biscuits* precisely because the dough was beaten extra long to insure that they would come out of the oven very moist and flaky. The waitress had observed from the first time she entered the café that Dee had a beautiful figure. She had also noticed that Henry had lost what she estimated to be twenty pounds since she first saw him. His weight loss had added significantly to his appearance. The waitress assumed that the two were having an extramarital affair.

Henry had chosen Daisy's Café because it was on the outskirts of town. He felt relatively secure that no one in his church or social circle would ever patronize the establishment. His Black BMW 7 Series was surrounded in the parking lot by old pick-up trucks and well-used automobiles. There was always one red Cadillac with personalized plates. They read simply, *Daisy*. At first he feared that his car would get the attention of a passerby that knew him. He started parking it behind the restaurant, out of view of the highway. He and Dee had been meeting here several times each week the past couple of months.

Dee looked up at Henry. "Henry, your hand feels so good."

Henry smiled. "I know. Your leg feels awfully good to my hand."

"Henry, are we ever going to sleep together?"

He chuckled. "I certainly hope so."

"Well, when?"

Henry stopped rubbing her leg and took her hand in his. "Dee, if I were most any other man I think we would probably have already made love several times. I just need you to be patient with me."

"Henry, we've been seeing each other for two months. I don't mind the sneaking around because I understand it's necessary. I know it's not going to be this way forever."

"Dee, Honey, please…it's just that I know what it is to be hurt and the last thing I ever want to do is hurt you. When I make love to you, you're going to know that it will be the beginning of our life together."

"You just need to know, Mister Mudd, that I really want you. I want you to make love to me."

"And you need to know just how nice that sounds to me. I just want us to do this the right way. I'm filing for a divorce against Virginia and I'm going to sue for full custody of my girls. It's going to get nasty. She doesn't know yet just how nasty it will get if she fights me. I can only hope for her sake and that of the girls she won't."

"And you don't want me involved."

"No, I don't. I love you. I don't want Virginia and her counsel to be able to implicate you in any way in my divorce. In fact, I was going to tell you today that I think we should not see each other again until my divorce is final."

"Oh, Henry, no. We can continue to be careful, can't we? No one has seen us so far."

Henry squeezed her hand. "We've been lucky, but I don't want to take any more risks. I'll not have you labeled as *the other woman* in Falls City. If that happens, you'll never be accepted at First Church or in Falls City Society. That would break my heart."

"You really do love me, don't you?"

"Dee, it's because I love you that we need to take our time and do this the right way. I need to get through my divorce and then there will be the appropriate time for me to introduce you to my friends. I want to be able to meet your friends and family as a single man. I don't want our life together to begin with any clouds over it."

"What about your girls, Henry? Will they accept me?"

Henry nodded. "Dee, it's going to be difficult for them. We're simply going to have to take our time. They're good girls and they'll come to love you, but it's not going to happen right away. Let's not make the mistake of trying to force our relationship on them."

"I know that you're right, but this is going to be so hard. Henry, I physically hurt when I'm not with you. My body aches. I think about you all the time. It's all I can do to keep from telling my friends about you. All of them keep asking me why I'm so happy. They already know that it's because I'm in love. They just don't know with whom."

A stern look crossed Henry's face. "Dee, you must not tell anyone about us. The only way two people can keep a secret is if one of them is dead. The news of our relationship would just be too delicious. So far we haven't done anything but some passionate kissing. I haven't been this restrained since I was a teenager in the back seat of my dad's Lincoln. But that won't matter if the gossips get hold of us."

"Oh, Henry, I haven't told anyone. I won't tell anyone. I know that you're right. I want to have the life with you that you're planning for us. I assume that means you want me to be your wife?"

A big smile crossed Henry's face. "Now, you wouldn't deprive a fellow the opportunity to propose in a proper manner, would you?"

"So this is not just a fling? I'm not your in-between person?" Dee was clearly looking for reassurance. She didn't want to be Henry's transitional woman that took him from marriage to the single life.

"Dee, this is real. I know that I love you. I don't want this to ever end. I'm miserable when I can't be with you. The only relief I can get is to hear your voice. I think the only way we're going to be able to stay away from each other until my divorce is final is to talk on the phone, but we've got to be careful." Henry reached into his inside coat pocket and brought out a plastic card. He handed it to Dee.

"What's this?"

"It's a prepaid telephone calling card. I don't want you calling me from your house or your work. Use this to call me from a pay phone, but make sure that no one is around to overhear our conversation. I'll do the same."

"Do you think this is really necessary?"

"Yes, Dee. I do." Once again he reached into his coat pocket and brought out a key. He handed it to her. "This is a key to a mailbox at a postal annex near the hospital. I've already paid for it in cash for the next three months. Check it every few days. We'll use it as a drop box. I'll want to write you some letters and cards and leave them in the box for you. But you have to promise me that once you've read them you'll shred them. Do not keep them. You can leave me cards and letters in that same mailbox. I kept a key for myself and will check it from time to time."

"Oh, Henry, this just seems over the top. I really don't think we have to do all this."

"Dee, I want us to begin our marriage untainted. If there's even the slightest hint that we had a relationship before I was divorced, you'll never be accepted as my wife by the people that matter in my life. We have to do this. There simply is no other way. I love you and I want this to work."

A tear dropped down Dee's cheek. "I know you're right. It's just going to be so hard."

Henry put his arm around her and drew her close to him. He wiped away her tear with his other hand. "Dee, I love you. We're going to make this work." He guided her face to his with his free hand and kissed her passionately.

"You two really should get a room." The waitress interrupted their kiss.

Henry and Dee both blushed. "That's just not an option for us, but we could use some privacy."

The waitress studied both of their faces. "My name's Daisy. I own this place. I don't think that you're going to get much privacy here. The lunch crowd is about to arrive." She took a drag from her cigarette while she studied their faces one more time. "I'll tell you what I will do.

I keep a guest house in back of the restaurant." She offered Henry a key. "Go on in. Make yourselves at home. Just bring me the key when you're finished."

Dee grabbed Henry's arm and squeezed. "Let's do, Honey. It's going to be a long time before we get to see each other again. Henry, please…"

Henry smiled at Dee and then at the waitress. He nodded and took the key from her. "Thanks. Thanks so much."

Chapter 5

"I THINK YOUR election is guaranteed." Ned Boone was having a difficult time keeping his excitement under control.

"You really think so, Ned?" Judith Idle beamed.

Ned had asked Elmer and Judith Idle to meet him in the grill at the Falls City Country Club. They had been some of the most outspoken critics of The Reverend Steele Austin's ministry. Together they had made several different plans to have him removed from office. To date all their efforts had been to no avail. Judith Idle was a part time employee on the parish staff. Elmer was a member of the Vestry. He was running for Senior Warden. His platform could be summarized in one statement that he repeated as frequently as possible to the right audience. "I'll make Steele Austin's life miserable. He won't be able to resign fast enough."

"What makes you so sure, Ned?" Elmer queried. "Austin has his supporters. They know I'm not a fan. I don't think they're going to simply sit back and let me become Senior Warden."

Ned made a calming motion with his hands. "Don't you worry about a thing. I've organized over thirty cottage meetings in this parish. I've been to every one of them. There are a lot of people in this congregation that just don't know the facts about this man. They've all promised to show up at the annual meeting. We're about to have the biggest voter turnout in the history of this parish. There's going to be people at this next meeting that have never attended a parish meeting. Take my word for it. Your election is a done deal."

Judith closed her eyes and lifted her hands in prayer, "Oh, thank you, Jesus. The day of our deliverance is at hand. Your flock will be protected from this false prophet." She then started whispering over and over, "Thank you, Jesus. Thank you, Jesus."

The waiter interrupted her prayers. "Is everything okay here? Do you need anything?"

"I suppose we should order." Ned responded.

"Are you familiar with the grill menu?"

Elmer raised his voice to the waiter. "Young man, I've been a member of this club my entire life. My parents and my grandparents were all members of this club. Mister Boone's family membership goes back to the founding of this club. They were charter members. I suggest that you get to know your membership before you start asking stupid questions. Of course, we know the grill menu."

The young man blushed. "I'm sorry. I've only been here a few days."

Ned Boone glared at the waiter. "That's a few days too long. I'll be stopping by the club manager's office on my way out of here today. While I don't have the authority to dismiss you, I can promise you that today is your last day."

The young man appeared to be on the verge of tears. "I'm so sorry. I wish you would give me another chance. I really need this job."

"You should have thought of that before you failed to inquire as to just who you would be serving today." Elmer was just as cold and abusive in his tone as Ned had been.

"Judith, please tell this imbecile what you want, but don't count on him getting it right. Would it be better if we wrote our orders down for you?" It was clear that Ned had no intention of giving the waiter a second chance.

After they had all ordered, Ned indicated for them to lean in closer. "I have an ace in the hole."

Judith smiled brightly. "Ned, you fox. I knew that you wouldn't leave all this to chance."

"As you know, it's the custom for the retiring members of the Vestry to be the tellers at the annual meeting. There are four members retiring this year. I've spoken to three of them. I have some information on each one of them that they would not want to have made public. They will work together to make sure that regardless of how the ballots are cast, Elmer will be elected by a clear majority."

Judith sat back in her chair. "Oh, Ned, I don't know. That doesn't seem right."

Elmer patted her on her hand. "Honey, unusual times call for unusual methods. We've simply got to insure that the parish is rid of this arrogant priest. You've got to think of the greater good. Sometimes the end does justify the means and this is one of them."

Just then the waiter returned with three sodas. "Mine is a diet soda. You did remember that?" Ned asked.

The waiter appeared flustered. He sat down the drinks in front of Judith and Elmer. He looked at Ned, "I'll be right back."

"Idiot!" Ned was exasperated. "You can't even get a simple drink order straight. I can't wait to see what you do with our meal."

The waiter scurried away and returned quickly with Ned's drink. "I'm so sorry."

"Sorry just won't do. " Elmer glared at the young man.

When the waiter had departed, Ned signaled for them all to lean in toward the center of the table once again. He looked around the room to make sure that no one was listening. Then he reached into the breast pocket of his suit coat and brought out three pictures. "Don't ask me how I came to have these. Just know that if all else fails, a copy of them will be in the mailbox of every member of First Church, as well as the newspaper and television stations."

Judith took the pictures. She shook her head and made shaming noises. "Ned, I'm not at all surprised. I've never trusted that blonde hussy. Steele Austin has been a fool to trust his wife. She just parades around shooting her single's bar stare at every man she sees. Do you know who the man is? He's got to be ten years younger than her. It's just a disgrace."

Elmer took the pictures from her and sorted through them twice. He gave a low whistle. "She looks awfully good in that bikini."

"Elmer Idle!" Judith rebuked. "I'm ashamed of you."

He reached over and put his arm around her. "Now, darling, you know you're the only woman for me. I was just observing that if a woman is going to walk around in a skimpy bathing suit like this, then she's inviting men to hit on her."

"Oh, she's a real flirt. She's been trolling for someone to take her bait from the day she moved to Falls City."

Elmer wrinkled his brow. "How are you going to know when to mail these pictures out, Ned?"

"Simple. Either Austin resigns or I mail out these photos. That's all there is to it."

Judith nodded. "I'm not so sure you shouldn't mail them out anyway."

A devious smile crossed Ned's face. "First, we get his resignation. Then we decide on whether or not to mail out the pictures. But I agree. She should be exposed for the slut that she is."

"Have you heard the rumors that Austin has hired a woman priest?" Elmer whispered.

"Those are not rumors. I called the Bishop's office and Canon Vernon confirmed it as fact. The announcement is going to be in the parish newsletter this week."

"Well, I just don't think women should be priests." Judith snorted. "And I certainly don't want a priestess at First Church. Priestesses have always been the temple prostitutes. Jesus would never have sabotaged his mission by having priestesses."

Ned Boone was amused by her response. "Don't worry about it. Once we make Elmer Senior Warden and we've gotten rid of Austin, we'll not only send the priestess packing, but we'll also rid the parish of that African that Austin is so fond of."

Elmer looked puzzled. "How are we going to do that? I don't know if that's possible, Ned."

"Oh, not only is it possible, but we'll have help from the Diocese. Canon Vernon said that he would work with us to make it happen."

"Sounds like you and the new Canon have become great friends." Elmer chuckled.

"Oh, we're more than friends. We had a long visit. He's supportive of everything we're trying to do. He can't wait to get rid of Austin and his entire clergy team. Vernon is a smart man. He wants to make sure that the only clergy that are brought into this Diocese are orthodox. He's a conservative and he wants all the priests in the Diocese of Savannah to be conservative as well."

"What about the Bishop?"

This time Ned couldn't contain his laughter. "Oh, the Bishop only thinks he's in control. Canon Vernon is running this Diocese. If necessary, that includes running the Bishop. We all know just how easily manipulated he is anyway. Have you all forgotten how we manipulated Rufus Petersen into defending the business manger, Ted Holmes? Then we convinced him to be suspicious of the Rector."

"I still think Ted was framed." Judith pouted.

"We all do, Honey. We all know that Austin is the crook and that he only framed poor Ted in order to cover up his own financial indiscretions. Ted was a good man that gave his all for this parish. It's just so wrong what the Rector has been able to get by with." Then Elmer started chuckling. "But it was fun to manipulate old Petersen. God, it was just too easy to get him all worked up. It didn't take much at all. The man's worst enemy is his own temper. And it sounds like the new Canon has figured out just which buttons to push in order to control him as well." With that, Elmer let out a roar of laughter. Judith and Ned, who also enjoyed a good laugh at the Bishop's expense, quickly joined him.

The waiter returning with their meals interrupted their laughter. He nervously placed a plate before each of them. "Will there be anything else?"

"Yes, you can prepare each of us one of the Mud Sundaes for desert. Do you think that you can do that without messing it up?"

The waiter was so humiliated that he couldn't even make eye contact with any of them. "Yes, I believe I can."

Ned started laughing again. "Do you hear that? He believes he can. Don't believe you can. Go back there and do it. But mark my word it will be the last thing that you ever serve in this club or any other club I'm a member of."

Tears rolled down the waiter's cheeks as he backed away from the table. He was able to compose himself by the time he got back to the kitchen. He began preparing the three Mud Sundaes. Then in a split second an idea came to him. He decided to make their Sundaes extra special. So just before pouring the chocolate syrup over their ice cream, he looked around. No one was watching. He made their Sundaes disgustingly special.

Chapter 6

"Now, STEELE, I'll not hear any excuses. Horace and I will expect you for lunch promptly at twelve noon at our home." Steele Austin had learned early in his ministry at First Church that you could send your regrets to a lot of people, but Almeda Alexander Drummond was not one of them. Almeda had led the charge to have Steele removed as Rector during his first year in Falls City. The tide began to turn in his favor with her when she allowed him to pastor her through her husband Chadsworth's suicide. Things really turned in his favor when she fell in love with his African American associate, Horace Drummond. Their romance and subsequent marriage had been the talk of Falls City for weeks. Almeda had paid a high price in Falls City society for her marriage. She was no longer invited to be a trainer for the Junior League. Her memberships at the Falls City Country Club and the Magnolia Club had been revoked. She was removed from the invitation list of some of the most exclusive social events, including the annual Magnolia Ball and the Cancer Benefit. Almeda knew that her former society companions would remain cordial because that is the Southern Way, but her entrée to Falls City Society would come to a conclusion once she married Horace. She didn't care. She was a woman in love.

After Almeda became so enamored with Horace, she redirected the very energy she had used to try to end Steele's ministry into defending him. In fact, she and Horace had become two of his and Randi's best friends. Steele really didn't feel like having lunch with anyone. He wished that there were a hole that he could climb into and then pull the hole itself in after him. His life was beginning to unravel. Someone had anonymously sent him photos of his wife in a compromising situation with another man. That alone had really hurt Steele. If Steele Austin had known anything beyond a shadow of a doubt, it was that he was destined to marry Randi. He worshipped her. There wasn't a thing in the world he wouldn't do for her if she asked. They had two beautiful children. He thought he had a charmed life with his little family. But the photos had planted doubts in his mind. He still didn't know who had sent them to him. He didn't recognize the young man. He just knew that if the pictures were to be believed, his wife was either being very flirtatious or she was, in fact, cheating on him. Just the thought of it made him so sick to his stomach that he had to force himself to eat. His sleep had become restless. He found it difficult to focus on work.

Steele turned his car onto River Street. It was the most exclusive street in Falls City. Anyone who was anyone in Falls City Society lived on this street. Everyone else wanted to. Not only did he feel like his marriage was falling apart, but now Elmer Idle was running for Senior Warden. Elmer had never tried to hide his disapproval of Steele's leadership style. Steele had made the mistake of putting his wife Judith on his staff. Even though she was part-time, she continued to undermine his ministry and leadership at every opportunity.

Steele pulled his car into the circular drive in front of Almeda and Horace's home. He really wasn't up for conversation. He laid his head back against the headrest in his car and closed his eyes. To top everything off, the Bishop that now supported his ministry had employed a passive aggressive Canon For Clergy Deployment. The Canon was actively working in the Diocese and First Church to undermine his ministry. Steele and Canon Vernon had already had two very angry encounters on the telephone. Steele dismissed him as a control freak, but he knew that he was dangerous.

A knocking on his car window interrupted Steele's thoughts. It was Horace.

"Are you okay, brother?"

Steele opened the door. "I was just resting my eyes for a few minutes. I have a slight headache."

Horace chuckled. "My friend, from where I sit it appears to me you have several headaches, and most of them are on the membership roll of First Church."

Steele patted Horace on the back. "I think you know me a bit too well."

"Come on in. Almeda has lunch prepared. I hope you're hungry. You know how she is."

"I fear I don't have much of an appetite."

"Well, you're on your own if you don't do justice to her food."

Steele smiled. "I'll give it my best effort."

Horace led Steele into the library. He was surprised to see Chief Sparks and Stone Clemons standing with a drink in their hands. "Is this going to be a drinking lunch, fellows?" Steele forced himself to smile.

Stone Clemons was one of the patriarchs of Falls City and First Church. He was well known throughout the state of Georgia. He was highly regarded. He had been one of Steele's strongest supporters from the day he arrived. "Faaa...thur." Stone always drew out the word when he addressed Steele. "Every lunch is a drinking lunch. Remember, that the Good Book instructs us to *drink a little wine for the stomach's sake.*"

"I'm sure that it does if you say so, but I don't believe that it says anything about Tennessee Bourbon Whiskey with a splash of branch."

"It's implied." Stone grinned.

"And Chief, are you drinking too? Is this your day off?"

"It is. And if I'd known I was going to have to spend part of it with this old reprobate, I would have started drinking at breakfast." The room filled with laughter. All knew that these two hunting and fishing buddies were inseparable. They had been friends longer than Steele had been drawing breath. The Chief had been a protector for Steele and his family. He'd provided security for them when their lives had literally been threatened. He was a progressive law enforcement officer for the Old South. He was first in the state to integrate his force. He was the first to employ women officers. He was the first to employ gay officers. His integrity was beyond question.

Almeda entered. She walked up to Steele and gave him a big hug accompanied with a kiss on the cheek. "I'm so pleased you could make it. I'm so pleased all of you could come. I've had a table prepared for us in the solarium. Please, bring your cocktails and follow me."

The solarium was just off the library. The room was filled with beautiful Cymbidium orchids of all colors. The glass windows and doors looked out over the expansive back yard that had a swimming pool as its centerpiece. The table was beautifully set to Almeda's usual standards of excellence. "I know that you all are busy men, so I've had a light lunch prepared. It should be filling enough to see you through the afternoon, but not so filling you'll need to take a nap."

Soon a young Asian boy dressed in a white jacket and black bow tie came into the solarium with a large silver bowl. He immediately began filling crystal soup bowls with Gazpacho. "Now I hope this will satisfy you, but not so much you won't have room for dessert. I've prepared something a little heavier for dessert, but I think you all can afford it, especially you, Steele. You are getting much too thin. I hope my red velvet cake will put a pound or two on you."

The meal conversation covered the usual male topics. Almeda had smiled through them all. The Atlanta Braves, fishing, hunting, and community politics were all argued with passion. After the cake and coffee had been served Almeda nodded at Stone. "I think it would be best if you began, Stone."

Steele looked around the table. All present were looking at him. "Faa…thur. This is an intervention."

Steele felt his forehead wrinkle involuntarily. "A what?"

"Faa…thur, we are your friends. We all love you. Some of us are old enough to love you as though you were our own child, but we're worried about you."

Steele was still having trouble digesting what was being said.

Horace put his hand on Steele's arm. "Brother, you've just not been yourself the past couple of weeks. Something is drastically wrong. We just want to know what we can do to help."

"Oh, it's just the usual church stuff. Nothing new." Steele shrugged.

"If there weren't a lady present, you know exactly what I'd call that last statement." Chief Sparks met Steele's eyes. The Chief had taken his signature cigar out of his jacket pocket and was chewing on it. He never lit the cigar. "Look at you. You look like you haven't slept in weeks."

"And you're getting thin as rail." Almeda chimed in.

"Brother, the entire staff is worried about you. You just don't seem to be present. It's as though you're constantly lost in thought or worry." Horace tried to comfort Steele.

"And..." Stone paused as though he were considering carefully the words he wanted to choose. "Quite frankly, Steele, your sermons haven't been up to their usual standard. Now tell us what's going on."

"Friends, I really don't have anything to tell you."

Chief Sparks took the cigar out of his mouth once again. He pointed at Steele with it. "Well, I've done some investigating on my own and I think I know exactly what's bothering you."

Steele felt his heart skip a beat. He was afraid that the Chief had somehow found out about Randi's indiscretions. He prepared himself for what he feared would be the most humiliating moment in his entire life. "It's Elmer and Judith Idle, isn't it?"

A strange feeling of relief washed over Steele. "What have you heard?"

"One of my officers discovered a couple of cars illegally parked over on Florida Street last week. He investigated and discovered that some people attending a church meeting owned them. One of the drivers told him that they were having a meeting to discuss a plan for getting rid of their preacher. The officer asked him which church he attended and he told him First Church. The officer reported it all to me because he knew that First Church is my church."

"What does that have to do with the Idles?" Steele asked.

"Stone and I've both made some inquiries. We've discovered that Ned Boone is organizing these meetings to discuss a campaign to get Elmer Idle elected as Senior Warden. We all know how both men feel about you."

Steele nodded.

Almeda took in a deep breath. "Well, Steele, that's the reason for this lunch. We want you to stop worrying about all this. You have a lot of supporters in this congregation and we're simply not going to sit by and put up with any more of Ned Boone's shenanigans. "

Stone leaned toward Steele and pointed his finger for emphasis. "You can take that to the bank. There are plenty of us that have had our fill of Ned Boone and the Idles. We're prepared to fight fire with fire. And this time they won't have the Bishop helping them."

"No, but they have the Canon to the Ordinary on their side. I'm afraid that he and I have already locked horns twice."

Horace squirmed in his seat. "I just don't know what the Bishop was thinking when he hired that man. He's never been to seminary. He's never been in charge of a congregation. His theological and management training are practically non-existent. He's an absolute control freak whose first priority is being in charge. It's his way or the highway. Clearly he has his own agenda. And most of the clergy know that he has an incredible ability to manipulate the Bishop. He'll tell half-truths or manufacture out and out lies in order to get the Bishop worked up to do his bidding. It's absolutely amazing. Every priest in this Diocese has already figured that they need to steer clear of his office."

"Well, that may be." Stone grinned. "But we're in charge of First Church and not Canon Vernon. We'll run First Church. We're the largest contributor to this Diocese and if he wants that to continue he'll not interfere in the decision making of the leaders of this congregation."

The only thing that Steele could think of was how to bring this luncheon to a conclusion. "I want to thank all of you. You've made me feel a lot better. I have a full afternoon of appointments, so I really need to get back to my office." Steele stood and the rest did the same.

"You are a very sweet and dear man, Steele." Almeda hugged him. "I want to thank you for coming today. We just wanted you to know that we love you and you have our support."

Steele smiled and started walking toward the door. At the door, he shook each of the hands and hugged Almeda one more time. "I love all of you and really appreciate your friendship and your support. Please don't worry about me. This has helped. I'm going to be just fine. Thank you, Almeda, for a wonderful lunch."

Steele tried not to run to his car. He was just relieved that none of them gave any indication that they knew about the pictures of Randi or any of her activities. A block from Almeda and Horace's house he whipped his car into an alley. He quickly threw open his car door and lost all his lunch. This was not a new experience for him. Since receiving the pictures of Randi he'd failed to keep much of anything in his stomach.

Back at the house, Stone and Chief Sparks were getting ready to leave. Almeda cooed, "Well, I think this was very worthwhile. I believe we were able to help him. I knew all along that he was upset over Ned Boone and the Idle's latest maneuverings."

Stone started to leave when his gaze fell on Chief Sparks. The Chief was chewing on his unlit cigar, lost in thought. "What are you thinking, Chief?"

The Chief continued to chew on his cigar before answering. "Just that I don't think that Boone and Idles are what has him worried. I don't believe he told us everything. In fact, I don't believe we even came near the truth today. There's something else. Something big. I just don't know what it is. And you know what? I don't think he's going to tell us or anyone else."

Chapter 7

"WHEN IS THE last time you had a full night's sleep, Steele?" Henry Mudd had been meeting weekly with Steele. He'd turned to Steele when he discovered that his wife, Virginia, was committing adultery. Like others in the parish, Henry had initially been one of the leaders opposed to Steele's ministry at First Church. And like several others, once they opened themselves to Steele and allowed him to pastor them through difficult situations, he had become one of Steele's strongest supporters.

"I just came from a lunch where some of my self-appointed parents gave me a lecture on slowing down and getting some rest."

"Well, I think maybe you'd better listen to them." Henry walked over to the couch and took his customary seat. Steele sat across from him in one of his wingback chairs. "Is baby Amanda keeping you up? Does she have colic?"

Steele forced a smile. "No, the baby is fine. Most nights she only wakes up one time. We feel real lucky."

"Well, whatever is bothering you is taking its toll on you. How much weight have you lost?"

Steele shrugged. "I don't know. I haven't weighed myself. I needed to take off a couple of pounds anyway."

"You've lost more than a couple of pounds. You're beginning to look like you have a serious disease. Have you been to a doctor?"

Steele held up both of his hands in front of him. "Okay, enough. Like I said, I've already received this lecture from one group, and I don't need to hear another."

Henry nodded. "If you say so. Just know that I'm here to help if there's anything you need."

"I appreciate that. Now, catch me up. Have you made any decisions?"

"I'm filing for divorce." Henry blurted.

"I felt like you were leaning that direction last time we talked. Did anything new happen to help you come to that conclusion?"

Henry looked around Steele's office. "Do you have a television and video player in here?"

"No."

"Do you have access to one?"

"I can have a sexton bring me one. We have several on carts that we can move from room to room."

"Would you mind having one brought in here? There's something I really want you to see. It will help you understand just why I've made the decision that there's no hope for my marriage to Virginia."

Within minutes a sexton knocked on Steele's door and rolled a cart into the office with a television and VCR on it. He plugged it in the wall outlet and then asked Steele if there was anything else he needed. Steele thanked him and he left, shutting the door behind him.

Henry turned on the television and put the tape in the VCR. "As you know, I already have videos and photos of Virginia with that French Frog. I also have tapes of their telephone conversations. Then, of course, you knew about her pregnancy and abortion. I was going to bite the bullet for my daughters' sake and just tough out some sort of amicable relationship with Virginia. But then…" Henry paused and took a deep breath. "My detective discovered what I'm about to show you. It's the final straw."

Henry hit the play button. A title page announced: *Naughty Housewives Uncovered.* He fast-forwarded through several scenes that clearly showed different people copulating. "Henry," Steele protested. "I'm not sure you want to show me this tape."

Henry paused the tape and looked at Steele. "I really need to show this to you. Please. I need you to understand."

"Henry, I don't need to see this tape. I do understand. I think you have already suffered more than any husband I've ever counseled with. You have my support."

Henry nodded. "I appreciate that, but I still want you to see this. I have to show it to someone. Showing it to you will take it from nightmare to reality for me. I trust you. I just need you to see it. We'll turn it off after just a few seconds."

Steele nodded reluctantly. Henry pushed the play button. The camera focused immediately on Virginia's face giving oral pleasure to a man. The camera panned back to show the man's face. "That's not the Frenchman!" Steele was shocked.

Henry paused the tape on the man's face. "Do you recognize him?"

Steele studied the man's face. "He does look familiar. Where have I seen him?"

"He's a two-bit actor down at the dinner theatre off Main Street."

Steele snapped his fingers. "That's where I've seen him. Randi and I have gone over there a couple of times. They do some slapstick and parodies on Falls City Society. First Church is often one of their targets. Do you think she knows she's being filmed?"

Henry moved the tape forward and then hit pause again. "Look at what's in his hand."

"It's a remote control."

"My detective's hunch is that she didn't know she was being recorded. If you were to watch the entire thing you'd notice that he's only holding the remote when she's not looking directly at him."

"How did you find this thing?"

"The actor had a stag party and showed the film to his guests. It just so happened that one of my detectives was one of the guests. He recognized Virginia." Henry gave Steele an exasperated look. "This thing is on the internet for the entire world to watch."

Steele turned to walk back to his chair. "Turn it off. I don't blame you, Henry. Enough is enough."

Henry reached out and grabbed Steele's arm. "Wait, there's one more." Once again Henry fast forwarded through several different scenes and then pushed the play button. It was a different room, a different bed and a different man, but it was Virginia. The camera did not change perspectives. It was fixed at one angle. Henry pushed the pause button. "Do you recognize this room?"

Steele blushed. "No, should I?"

"Not necessarily. This is our bedroom. This is the bed that Virginia and I made love in. Our children were conceived in this bed."

"Do you know this guy?"

Henry nodded. An angry look crossed his face. "This is the contractor that I hired to do some remodeling on our house."

Steele gave a low whistle. "Man, that's low. It doesn't look like either one of them knew they were being filmed."

"I agree. I don't know who hid the camera in our bedroom. My detective's hunch is that it was the man's wife because she has already filed divorce papers on him."

Henry ejected the tape and unplugged the equipment. He walked over to the windows in Steele's office to look out. "I'm a really stupid man, Steele. There was a point in all of this that I'd tried to convince myself that I could excuse one indiscretion. But three! Or God only knows how many more. I just can't. I don't think any man in his right mind could forgive this."

"Has she been served with the divorce papers?"

"It's happening while we speak."

"I'm sorry, Henry. I'm really sorry this has happened to you. You don't deserve this. No man deserves anything like this."

Henry walked to the couch and sat down. "I don't have any tears left. I really don't have any anger left either. I just want to bring all of this to an end."

Steele nodded. "I understand. Your detective has done some outstanding work for you. What's his name?"

Henry tossed Steele a surprised look. "Do you need a detective, Steele?"

Steele pretended to chuckle. "No, but from time to time we need to do a background check on teachers in the school, nursery attendants and youth workers."

"I thought you already had an agency you worked with."

"We do. I just thought it wouldn't hurt to have a back up."

Henry studied Steele's face. "If you say so. I'll have my secretary send you one of his business cards."

After Henry left, Steele went back to his desk and took out the envelope containing the pictures of Randi. He took them out and studied them one more time. He knew that he needed to get to the bottom of these photos. It would be better for him not to use the agency the church and school employed. The detectives knew him and Randi too well. He would use the agency that had done the work for Henry.

Chapter 8

"STEELE, WHERE HAVE you been? It's so late. Why are you just now getting home?" Randi was putting Amanda in her crib. She was sleeping soundly. Steele leaned over and kissed Amanda on the forehead.

"I was working late."

"Steele, I tried to call your office several times on your private line. There was no answer."

"Oh, I guess I had the *Do Not Disturb* button on."

Randi was trying to control her worry and her anger. She walked across the hallway into the master bedroom. Steele followed her. She sat down on the edge of the bed. "Steele, have I done something? What's wrong? Please tell me what's bothering you."

Steele shrugged. "What makes you think something is wrong?"

Tears sprang to Randi's eyes. "I feel like you've been avoiding me. Travis hasn't seen you in almost a week. You leave before he wakes up in the morning and you don't get home until after he's asleep. You haven't even held your daughter in over a week. Steele, they miss you. I miss you. Now, what's going on?"

Steele started removing his clerical collar. He took off his clerical shirt and stood shirtless at the edge of the bed. "Randi, I've just got a lot on my mind. I have a lot to do. I've been trying to put a sermon together for this Sunday and the words just aren't coming to me. There's nothing else wrong."

"Steele, do you realize that we haven't made love since the night before Amanda's baptism? That's the longest we've ever gone without making love. I need you. I want to feel close to you."

"Randi, I told you I have a lot on my mind. I just don't have the energy. I just need some space so that I can focus on my work."

Randi stared at her husband. She looked for some expression in his face that would help her understand him. "Steele, I'm sorry. That's just not like you. You've never let work keep you from the children and me. You've always found a way to make time for us."

Steele really didn't want to have this conversation. "Will you please try to understand? I feel like I'm being pulled in a thousand different directions. I really need you to just let me work my way through everything."

Randi wiped tears from her cheeks with her hands. She sat silently looking up at her husband. "Steele, if I've done anything to hurt you." She paused to take in a deep breath. "I'm so sorry. I didn't mean to. Please tell me what I've said or done."

Steele swallowed. He thought about asking her about the pictures, but decided against it. "Randi, I don't know how many ways I can explain to you that my plate is full to overflowing. I just need to be able to get some things done."

Once again Randi studied Steele's face. "Steele, do you still love me?"

Steele wanted this cross-examination to end. "Randi, that's a silly question. Of course I love you."

Randi felt a sense of relief wash over her. She stood and walked up to Steele. She put her arms around Steele's neck and kissed him on the lips. She squeezed up next to him. He put his arms around her waist. When she had finished kissing him, she left one hand around his neck and she placed the other hand on his chest. "Are you in the mood now, Cowboy?"

When Randi placed her hand on Steele's chest, the picture of her doing the same thing to the young man in the photo flashed into his mind. He pushed away from her. "I can't. I have to preach on Sunday and I'm simply not ready. It's a really important sermon. It will be Ginnifer Graystone's introduction to the congregation." He removed his hands from around her and turned to the dresser. He pulled out a t-shirt and pulled it over his head.

Randi tried once again by putting her arms around him. "I promise I'll be gentle."

Steele looked at her. "I really, really need you to understand. I've got to go work on this sermon. I'll go down to my study so I won't keep you awake." Then he kissed her on the cheek and pulled her arms from his waist. He walked out of the room. He stopped at Travis' bedroom. He covered him with the blanket he'd kicked off his bed. Then he went down to the study. He didn't turn on the light. He just sat in the darkness.

Upstairs, Randi lay in the darkness as well. She felt like her world was coming apart. She curled up into a fetal position on her bed. She reached over to where Steele usually slept. The bed felt so empty without him. She missed him. Once again, tears streamed down her cheeks and onto her pillow.

Chapter 9

THE FOLLOWING ARTICLE appeared in the Sunday morning Falls City Newspaper.

Woman Priest Arrives At First Church

The Reverend Ginnifer Graystone will become the first woman to celebrate Mass in the Episcopal Diocese of Savannah. She joins the staff of First Church under the leadership of the Rector, The Reverend Steele Austin. Since Father Austin's arrival at First Church, he continues to shake the foundations of the traditional parish with a new and innovative ministry style. He is noted for his controversial role in starting the local Soup Kitchen and Free Medical Clinic, among other community projects.

Bringing a woman priest to the staff of First Church is compatible with Father Austin's leadership style. However, not everyone in the Diocese of Savannah and First Church is welcoming her. We contacted the Bishop's office in Savannah. While the Bishop was not available, The Reverend Canon Jim Vernon received our call and offered the following comments. "As you know, there are great portions of the Episcopal Church that do not recognize women clergy. Not everyone in the Diocese of Savannah will warmly receive the latest innovation by the Rector of First Church. The Bishop of our Diocese has agreed to receive her and authorize her ministry, but I fear she has a rough road ahead of her."

When asked about the validity of her ordination, Canon Vernon offered the following. "This is an ongoing discussion in the Episcopal Church. As you know, the Roman Catholic Church and Orthodox

Christianity won't even discuss it. It's really quite simple. In every sacrament there's the outward and visible matter and the inward grace. The visible matter in baptism is water. The inward grace is reception into the Body of Christ. Since the time of Jesus the outward matter for ordination is male flesh. Male flesh is not the same as female flesh. Many in the Episcopal Church want to debate whether or not women should be priests. For the majority of us there is nothing to discuss. It's really quite simple. Women cannot be priests. The outward matter for the sacrament of the priesthood is male flesh. Women are excluded."

Elmer Idle is a member of the Vestry at First Church and is a candidate for the office of Senior Warden, or chief lay leader, in the congregation. He was equally adamant about the reception of a woman priest. "From ancient times women who functioned as priests were called priestesses. As you know they were the temple prostitutes. Did Father Austin happen to mention to you that Reverend Graystone is divorced? That makes it even more difficult for many of us to approve of her ministry. I fear that Father Austin will find that his latest departure from traditional Christianity will not be received by the vast majority of us at First Church."

Father Austin looks on the addition of The Reverend Graystone as an opportunity to expand the ministry offerings of the parish. He issued the following statement. "Women, by virtue of their creation, bring gifts to ministry that men do not possess. They are gifts given by the Creator. While Jesus did conform to many of the practices of His time, He challenged others. Through the centuries the Church has challenged traditions that no longer serve the greater good. The Episcopal Church has spoken quite clearly on the ministry of women priests and bishops. Our ministry is already so much richer because of the gifts that all these women have brought to us. We are learning that God values that which is on a person's heart much more than simply having a *Y Chromosome*. Change is always difficult. Change is always resisted. It is my prayer that the people of First Church and those in the Diocese of Savannah will open themselves to the ministry of Mother Graystone. If they do so, they will be richly blessed."

The Reverend Graystone will preside today at the eleven o'clock Mass at First Church. There will be a reception on the church grounds to welcome her and her two daughters.

Chapter 10

"No, YOU MAY not. You will address me on formal occasions as Mrs. Gordon Smythe. I choose always to honor my husband. It is a wife's duty to honor and respect her husband. The Bible is quite clear on this. I took sacred marriage vows and promised both God and my husband I would do that very thing. Informally, you may call me Mrs. Smythe. And while we are at it, let me make it clear that I'll have nothing to do with this *Mother* nonsense. Nor do I plan to call you *Reverend*. I will call you Mrs. Graystone. I am not a feminist and I will not call you *Miz* either. I trust I make myself clear on these matters."

Steele turned the corner into the Altar Guild sacristy just in time to see a very red-faced Ginnifer Graystone pulling herself away from Mrs. Gordon Smythe's stare. He put his arm around her shoulder and escorted her into the priest's vesting room. "I should have warned you. She really is a wonderful woman, but she has some very strong opinions on certain things."

Ginnifer nodded. "Boy, that was really something."

"I did tell you that you were coming to a parish in transition."

"You didn't tell me that it was a parish moving from the eighteenth century to the nineteenth." At that they both chuckled.

"I fear you may be more right about that than you realize." Steele started vesting. "Our custom is to have the celebrant wear a cope into the service and change into the chasuble at the offertory. The Altar Guild will put the chasuble on the communion rail for you if that's acceptable."

"That's fine." Ginnifer smiled. "I want to conform to the parish custom."

"That's great. The clergy crucifer and torchbearers will meet us here at the sacristy door and lead us into the nave. We'll follow them to the back of the church where the choir and other ministers will be waiting on us. " With that, Steele opened the door to the waiting crucifer and torchbearers. The organist began a long introduction to the opening hymn. They processed up the side aisle and paused at the baptismal font. The first thurifer started processing down the center aisle. The choir crucifer and torches followed. Then Steele was surprised to see that, standing on the other side of the choir, were a group of teenage girls all carrying banners. The girls all wore pink blouses and pink headbands. The banners were all made of pink cloth. A quick look at the banners and he realized they were each in honor of a female saint. The first young woman fell in behind the crucifer. She was carrying a banner to St. Cecilia, the patron saint of musicians. Then the choir began to process down the aisle. After every fourth choir member one of the banner bearers would enter and process down the aisle carrying the banner to yet another woman saint. There were banners to St. Joan of Arc, St. Monica, St. Clare, and St. Martha.

Steele whispered to the Verger. "Where did the banners come from?"

"The teenagers decided that they wanted to make a statement this morning. They did a study of women saints and made these banners to process. They asked me if they could. I figured you'd agree. "

"Nice work."

When all the banners and choir had passed, the second thurifer started down the aisle. The clergy cross and torches followed. The lay ministers entered the long procession. The Verger nodded for Ginnifer to pass. Steele put out his arm to stop her. He whispered to the Verger, "No, she is the celebrant. She will process last. Horace and I will process together. You lead her to the altar."

Steele started down the aisle and then glanced back over his shoulder. Immediately behind him walked a smiling teenage girl carrying a banner to St. Mary, the Mother of Jesus. When they arrived at the altar, Ginnifer took the thurible from the thurfier and blessed the altar with beautiful precision and grace. Steele looked out at the congregation. The ushers had allowed those standing outside to enter the nave. They were now standing all along the walls of the church and overflowing the baptismal area into the narthex and out onto the front lawn. He didn't recognize a lot of the people. He figured the article in the morning newspaper had brought out the curious. They were here in force.

After the reading of the Gospel, Steele climbed the steps to the pulpit. "This is a pivotal day in the life of First Church. Today, for the first time in our history, a woman will preside at the sacred table. It is my fervent prayer that you will welcome The Reverend Ginnifer Graystone and her daughters to this parish family." His words were met with a sprinkling of polite applause.

"I think it is important this morning that I devote my sermon time to doing a quick look at the role women played in scripture and the ministry of Jesus. Mind you, I will not be able to mention all the women in the scriptures. I will leave out more than I mention. I just think it is important that we remember the contributions of women in the history of our salvation. We tend to forget that the Book of Genesis has two creation narratives. We men tend to favor the story that has us created first and then woman being created from our rib. We often pervert the theology of that story to illustrate that women are to be subservient to men. There is a second story. A story that has men and women created at the same time. The significant description in this story is that God created them both, male and female, in His image. They were created equally and the charge to care for the garden was given to both of them."

Steele could see that his words were causing a few to squirm in their pews. "Women played a critical role in the ministry of Jesus. Jesus discussed his mission and ministry with the woman at the well. Jesus allowed himself to be anointed by a woman and reminded all the men present that she would be remembered for what she had done. Jesus healed the woman with the blood disease, he came to the aid of the woman caught in adultery, and healed a woman on the Sabbath. Jesus illustrated the love of God as tirelessly seeking the lost as a woman looking for a lost coin. "

Steele paused to study the worshippers. It was difficult to get a read on what they were thinking, but clearly he had their attention. "Would it surprise you to know that Jesus described himself as a female? We must not forget that he spoke of himself as a mother hen wanting to gather all of Jerusalem to herself. And finally, we must not forget that when all the disciples but John had forsaken Jesus on the cross, the women stayed with him. And just as the news of his birth was made possible by a woman, so the news of his resurrection was first carried by a woman."

Steele leaned over the pulpit so he could better look out at the congregation. "Now, let me bring all this home to you here at First Church. For the past two centuries, in this very parish, women have worked behind the scenes to prepare the holy table for us each Sunday. They arrive at the church early in the morning long before any of the rest of us. They lovingly spread the table linens on the altar. They freshen the flowers and insure the candles will light. They lovingly count the wafers and measure the wine to insure that none of us will leave the altar unfed. And when the service is over, they remain and continue their work while the rest of us are enjoying our Sunday dinner. All of the vessels must be washed. The flowers must be dismantled and rearranged in several individual containers to take to the sick in the hospitals. The priest's vestments and the altar linens must be carefully stored away. Those who work so tirelessly to insure that our services are worthy offerings to the Almighty are all women. But today there will be a change in our ministry together. A woman will stand at the holy table that has been lovingly prepared by other women and bless the holy food for all of us to eat and drink."

Steele turned to look at Ginnifer sitting in the Celebrant's chair. "Today, Mother Graystone is a visual reminder to us from God that in Jesus Christ there is neither Jew or Greek, slave or free, male or female. In Jesus Christ we are one in body and one in spirit. There are no second-class citizens. There is no inferior ministry. For He created them male and female in His own image and He gave the responsibility to care for the Garden to both of them equally."

Steele looked out at the congregation. Then he turned so he could look once again at Ginnifer. "Mother Graystone, we welcome you to First Church and this family of Jesus Christ." With those words the teenagers that had been carrying the banners sprang to their feet and began applauding. Soon more members of the congregation stood and joined in the applause. There were many, however, that remained seated and unmoved.

Steele thought all was going well until it came time to administer the sacrament. He was on one side of the communion rail. Ginnifer was on the other. He looked up to notice something very disconcerting. He noticed that the vast majority of the congregation was refusing to receive communion from Ginnifer. Even though the ushers were directing them to Ginnifer's line at the communion rail, they would simply move over to the line going to Steele's side of the altar. "Please, God." Steele prayed. "Don't let this happen." Nothing changed. The worshippers continued to come to his side of the rail. Then, to Steele's amazement, his prayer was answered in a way he never thought possible. The entire Altar Guild that was present had all gone to the sacristy and put on their Altar Guild smocks. Led by Mrs. Gordon Smythe and Mrs. Howard Dexter, they joined the line to receive communion from Mother Graystone.

Steele was beginning to relax when he heard Ginnifer shout, "Ouch!" Steele quickly looked her direction to see a man he'd never seen before biting Ginnifer's hand. Steele started moving toward the man when he quickly stood and ran from the altar rail and out the transept door. Steele reached Ginnifer and grabbed her hand. "Are you okay?"

She nodded tearfully. "I can finish giving communion."

Steele smiled, "I think you'd better go to the hospital and get a tetanus shot after the service."

She smiled back at him, "I was thinking rabies."

Chapter 11

THE RECEPTION TO welcome The Reverend Ginnifer Graystone was held on the parish grounds. It began with the all too familiar routine. First came the opportunity to photograph Steele and Ginnifer. Then the photographic patterns were predictable. Ginnifer and her daughters; Steele, Ginnifer, and Horace; and then Ginnifer, Steele and Randi, Horace and Almeda posed. Following the photographs, several members of the congregation formed a line to greet Ginnifer.

Steele was drawn into the part of these gatherings that he found exhausting. Invariably one or two predictable members that had been meaning to talk to him would corner him. They had an idea on how he could do things better, or couldn't they go back to the old way of doing things. There were the usual complaints about the choice of hymns, the loudness of the organist's playing, and the noisy children in church.

When he was able to get a look around the reception, he was pleased to see that several teens had surrounded Ginnifer's daughters and were making them feel welcome. He was also pleased that the line to greet Ginnifer was still quite long. He started to go to the buffet table to get something to eat. He began filling his plate when he felt a tap on his shoulder. "Father Austin, I really need to talk to you. It's important." He put his half filled plate back on the table to follow the woman to a more secluded part of the reception. He knew he'd have to stop at a drive through on the way home in order to get something to eat. But then, that was a familiar routine as well.

"Let me tell you." Steele knew what was coming next. "I've got this problem. I've been meaning to call your office for an appointment, but this has just been eating me up."

Steele would listen for a few minutes and then repeat the ever so familiar, "You're right. You need to call my office for an appointment. We can't possibly deal with your dilemma here. Call my office and you'll have my undivided attention. It will also insure that we'll not be interrupted." That scenario would repeat itself several times during the course of the reception. It always did. Steele also knew that most of them would never call for an appointment.

Chief Sparks approached him. He pointed back over his shoulder with his customary unlit cigar. "Looks to me like there's a big powwow going on over there by the magnolia."

Steele looked in the direction of the magnolia tree. Huddled together were Ned Boone, Elmer and Judith Idle, and two other couples. The two couples were listening to Elmer Idle. There faces were contorted in disbelief. "I've got a hundred dollar bill in my wallet that says he's not praising you for your leadership style."

Steele just shook his head. "You know, Chief, that's become the new buzz phrase for criticizing clergy. *We don't like his leadership style.* I'm quite sure that we'll hear those words from Elmer and his followers on numerous occasions in the future."

The Chief put the cigar back in his mouth and started chewing on it while he studied the group by the magnolia. Then he took the cigar out of his mouth again, "Preacher, you may be right about that, but you have the pecking order all wrong. The cock of the walk over there is Ned Boone. He's the brain in the outfit. Elmer is just his mouthpiece."

Steele nodded.

"Are you boys making a battle plan?" Stone Clemons joined them.

"No, we're just watching the loyal opposition recruit new troops." Steele smiled.

Stone chuckled. "Padre, you are a lot more charitable than I am. I can think of a lot of names for that trio over there, but loyal opposition is not one of them."

"Stone, we've got to do something about that group." Chief Sparks whispered.

A devilish look crossed Stone's face. "Don't you have some sharp shooters over there at the police station?"

The Chief smiled, "I was thinking the bomb squad might be more effective."

"Well, use whatever you want, but Ned, Elmer and that entire crew over there need to be brought down a notch. "

Just then yet another person needing to talk to Steele tapped him on the shoulder. By the time he'd pointed out that they needed to make an appointment, Stone and the Chief had left the reception.

Steele spotted Henry Mudd and his two daughters. He walked toward them. Henry smiled and embraced Steele. "I'm putting that business card you asked me about in your coat pocket. I've told the detective you might need his services some time. I told him to give you a good rate."

"Thanks." Steele greeted Henry's two daughters. The oldest daughter had really changed her appearance. She had double pierced her ears. She had on bright lipstick and eye makeup. She was wearing tight clothes that left little to the imagination. Her fingernails were painted with black polish. She was polite but sullen, and totally uninterested in talking to Steele. The youngest had doubled her size since Steele had last seen her. Her clothes were tight, but for another reason. Steele couldn't help but think that each of the girls was responding to their parents' divorce in different ways. The oldest was rebelling against her mother always dressing them in Laura Ashley. The youngest was anesthetizing her pain with food. Steele was quite sure that Laura Ashley did not make clothes in her new size. He didn't blame Henry for the choice he'd made, but no one should ever fool themselves into thinking that divorce doesn't hurt the children as well.

There were just a few people remaining at the reception. Steele looked around for Randi. She was not to be seen. In fact, he hadn't seen her since they had their photograph taken with Ginnifer over an hour ago. He remembered Henry telling him Virginia would disappear at receptions and parties and he wouldn't be able to find her. A cold sweat broke out on his forehead. Then he thought she might have gone to the nursery to pick up Travis and Amanda. He entered the parish house and started walking down the hallway toward the nursery when he heard Randi laughing. He turned to see her standing in a dark stairwell with another man. Steele felt his stomach turn. Randi looked Steele's direction.

"Oh, Steele. Come here. There's someone I want you to meet."

Steele walked toward them, studying their body language for any hint of intimacy. He studied the man. He was not the same man that was in the photograph. The man in the photograph had a swimmer's build. This man was definitely in shape. He looked more like a body builder with broad shoulders, thick arms and a narrow waist. "Randi, I've been looking for you."

"Steele, this is Chuck. His son is in the play group with Travis." Steele shook the man's hand. He studied his face. He had a square face. Steele couldn't imagine that Randi would find him attractive. "It's nice to meet you. Randi, have you picked up the kids?"

"No, I was just on my way to do that when I ran into Chuck here. We've just been standing here talking."

"Well, it's nice to meet you, Chuck. Will you excuse us? We really need to get our children home."

Randi smiled at Chuck and then, to Steele's surprise, she put her arms around his neck and hugged him. Steele didn't know if he was feeling surprise or disgust. "I'll see you at the next play day."

Steele took Randi's arm and pulled her toward the nursery. "Steele, are you okay? What's wrong with you?"

Steele looked at his wife's face. "Nothing, I just think we need to get the children home. I need to take a nap. I'm tired." As they walked down the hall toward the nursery, Steele put his hand in his coat pocket. He felt for the card. It was there. He'd make the call first thing in the morning. He needed to know if his wife was just another Virginia Mudd.

Chapter 12

"THANKS, I'LL MEET you here in my office at four o'clock this afternoon." Steele hung up the telephone and read the business card one more time.

R &T Marital Investigations
For Your Own Peace of Mind
You Need to Know.

Steele had not had any peace in his heart or mind since the envelope containing suggestive pictures of his wife with another man had arrived at his office. The photos had only planted suspicion in him. He didn't know anything for sure. He only knew that he had not felt the same about Randi since they had arrived. It made him sick to his stomach to think that she was being unfaithful to him. He wanted to trust her, but these photos had changed all that. The motto on the business card was correct. He needed to know. He couldn't imagine divorcing Randi. He didn't want to split up his family. A tear slid down his cheek as he thought about the effects that a divorce would have on Travis and Amanda. He put the card in his desk drawer and whispered. "I've just got to find out if it's true."

Just then his intercom rang. He pushed the button. It was his secretary, Crystal. She whispered, "Father Austin, pick up the receiver." Steele did as she requested. "Father Austin, there are two police officers in my office. They are looking for you."

"Oh. Did they say what they wanted?"

"No, they just said that it was urgent. They need to speak to you right away." Crystal paused and lowered her voice even further. "Father Austin, I think they're identical twins. And…"

"Yes."

"Father Austin," he could hardly hear her. "Father Austin, they're black."

Steele knew immediately who they were. He decided to have some fun with Crystal. "Well, I don't guess they can help the twin thing, but do you think they've always been black or are they just trying to be fashionable?"

"Father Austin!" Crystal gasped.

"I'll be right out. I know who they are." Steele opened the door between his office and Crystal's. He extended his hand to the officers. "Hey guys, great to see you. It's been too long. Come on in. Can I get you some coffee?"

"No, Father Austin, but thanks for the offer." The two officers followed Steele into his office.

"How's your grandmother?"

The two men looked down at the floor. Then one of them met Steele's eyes. "That's why we're here, Father. She's real sick. The doctor says she's dying."

Steele motioned for the two men to sit down. They shook their heads. "I'm really sorry to hear that. I don't have to tell you just how much I loved your granddaddy, Willie. He was much more than a sexton here at First Church. He was my friend. And of course, you know that I love your grandma as well."

"She wants to see you before she dies."

"Of course, and I'll want to see her. Is she at the hospital?"

"No, Father. She wanted to die at home. We've had hospice nurses taking care of her. They've just been wonderful."

"When would be a good time for me to drop over and visit?"

The two men looked at each other. "Father Austin, I don't think you understand. We've come to carry you over to my grandma's house. Father, the nurse says it won't be much longer."

"Of course, then let's go. Just let me tell my secretary." Steele pushed the intercom. "Crystal, I have to go with these officers. I may be gone most of the day, but I should be back for my four o'clock appointment."

"Is everything okay?"

"Everything is under control. Don't worry about a thing. I'll see you later."

Steele got in the back seat of the squad car. The two officers drove him out of the church parking lot just as Judith Idle was getting out of her car. A shocked look crossed Judith's face.

The front yard and porch was filled with people. Steele estimated that there must be at least forty people standing in small groups. He exited the car and followed the officers into the tiny house past a few more folks sitting in the living room. He could see some women working in the kitchen placing food on the counter and table. When they entered Grace's bedroom, The Reverend Josiah Williams immediately greeted him. Steele had helped him do Willie's funeral. Since then the two men had become good friends. They had worked on several community projects together. He greeted Steele in his deep baritone voice, "Steele, I'm so glad you could come." Steele nodded and the two men embraced. "You remember my Rubidoux?"

"Yes, of course I do." Steele embraced her and kissed her on the cheek. Rubidoux was a flashy dresser. She didn't disappoint anyone on this occasion. Steele walked toward the hospital bed. Grace looked so tiny in the big bed. He glanced at the hospice nurse. She forced a smile and shook her head. Steele looked back at Josiah. He saw that Grace's two grandsons were standing with their wives. They were each holding a baby. Josiah walked over to the other side of the hospital bed. He took Grace's hand. "Grace, open your eyes. I want you to see who has come to see you."

Grace's eyes opened slightly and then a smile crossed her face. "Father Steele, I so wanted to see you."

Steele took her hand in his. He leaned down and kissed her on the cheek. "Grace, you sent two of the biggest officers at the Falls City Police Department to pick me up, but I would've come anyway."

"Just look at them, Father Steele. Willie and me so proud 'dem boys. You know we raised 'em as our own. Their mother was kilt in a car wreck when they were still small. Now, look at 'em. They fine policemen. And look at their beautiful wives. Those two girls just spoil ol' Grace. They treat me just like I was their own momma."

Steele nodded. "You have every right to be proud of these men. And no one deserves being spoiled more than you."

Grace let go of Steele's hand and pointed at the boys once again. "And those are my great-grandbabies. Can you believe those girls had their babies on the same day? Those precious girls blessed me with great-grandchildren."

"They're beautiful, Grace."

Grace began coughing and the hospice nurse wiped her mouth. "I's got to go home today, Father Steele. My Willie's been waiting on me far too long. I just know he's anxious to hold me in his arms again. Oh, I have so many folks over there waiting on me. My momma and daddy been gone so long. And these boys' momma. I needs to tell her all about her sons. She's gonna be so proud."

Grace started coughing again. The nurse once again wiped her mouth. Grace closed her eyes. The room was filled only with the sounds of her deep breathing. Steele took her hand once again. Everyone stood in silence. Then from the other room Steele heard humming. The humming grew louder as the people standing on the porch and yard joined in. Grace opened her eyes. "You hear that, Father Steele? That's my church. They all come to sing ol' Grace home. They good people. They my family. We take care of each other in the black church. Yo' white folks down at First Church could learn some things from us."

Steele nodded. "I fear you just might be right."

Grace nodded and closed her eyes. She squeezed Josiah's hand and then she squeezed Steele's hand. "Just can't wait to see if the Lord be black or if he be white." A smile crossed her face. The humming turned into song, *The gates opening wide...The gates opening wide...The gates opening wide for me. Gonna see Jesus. Gonna see my Lord. His arms wide open. He's running to meet me.* Then to Steele's surprise, all those singing began rhythmically clapping their hands. Steele looked over at Josiah. He had his eyes closed in prayer. Rubidoux came to the bed and put her arm around her husband's waist. She lifted the other hand toward the heavens. She too closed her eyes and began to whisper prayers. Steele looked back at Grace. It was then he realized she was not breathing. He motioned for the nurse. The nurse put her fingers on Grace's neck. She then nodded at Steele. "She's gone."

Steele felt his eyes fill with tears. He turned to look at her grand-sons. They were holding their wives. All of them were embraced in grief. Loud sobs came from the boys. It was a strange sight to see the women comforting their husbands through their own tears. Steele looked back at Grace and then he looked at Josiah, "May I?"

Josiah smiled. "Please."

Steele made the sign of the cross over Grace. "Depart out of this world Christian soul in the name of God who created you. In the name of Jesus who redeemed you. In the name of the Spirit that sanctified you. May the saints and angels come out to greet you and lead you into the holy city, Jerusalem. May your rest be this day in paradise and your dwelling in the household of God."

Chapter 13

"I DON'T THINK he loves me anymore."

Almeda handed Randi a tissue. "Now listen to me. That's just not the case. If I know anything, it's that Steele Austin is head over heels in love with you."

"Then what can it be? I've lost all the weight I gained with Amanda, but that doesn't seem to be enough."

"Enough?"

"Almeda, he hasn't touched me in almost a month. When I try to approach him he turns away. He's never been like that. We've always had a passionate love life."

Almeda sat back in her seat and took another sip of her tea. Randi had telephoned earlier and asked to come over. Almeda could tell by the tone of her voice that she was upset. She was glad that Randi had chosen to confide in her. "Randi, I need to tell you that several of us have been concerned about Steele for some time now. We just don't think he's himself. He seems so distracted."

"I know. It's been so long since I've even seen him smile. He used to laugh all the time. We used to laugh together. Almeda, he hasn't played with the children for weeks. When he's home he just seems to be in such a bad mood. He just wants us all to leave him alone."

Almeda nodded. "That certainly is compatible with what we've observed."

"What do you think it is?"

Almeda patted Randi's hand. "Well, I'm positive it's not you. Horace and I think that Steele knows he's under attack again from the Idles and Ned Boone."

Randi shivered. "Oh, I wish I'd never heard of any of them. They've just been awful to us. They're definitely clergy killers. Steele can't do anything right when it comes to them. I don't know how he can even stand to look at them."

"Well, it's time that the rest of us came to his aid. We're not going to let that group run off the best priest this parish has ever had."

Randi looked down at the tissue she was holding and started pulling at it. She was tearing it into small pieces. "So you really don't think that I'm the problem?"

Almeda smiled. "Steele loves you. He's absolutely devoted to you and to those children. Horace has told me on more than one occasion that he knows that Steele loves the Lord, but the Lord has some tough competition. He absolutely worships the ground that you walk on, Randi."

"Then why won't he talk to me? Why won't he make love to me? It's as though he can hardly look at me."

"Horace shared with me a time that he was under attack by a small group of so-called Christians. He remembers just how energy draining it was. He said that he felt completely debilitated. He felt like he was doing hand-to-hand combat with the devil and the devil was winning. He remembers thinking that he'd lost his soul. They were so vicious in their attacks on him that he just withdrew into himself. He didn't even want to be around the people in the parish that supported him. He said he got paranoid. He didn't know who his friends were and who was out to attack him. He said he became a zombie just going through the motions of ministry."

Randi's eyes brightened. "That's exactly how Steele is acting."

"I know. That's what Horace thought as well. That's why he told me about his own experience. "

"So you really don't think I have anything to worry about?"

"I think we all need to be concerned about Steele."

"Can we do anything about the Idles and Ned?"

Almeda shook her head. "I think they're beyond redemption. They just want their own way. They don't care what they're doing to Steele or what their actions will do to this church. They just want to be in control."

"What do you think I should do to help Steele?"

Almeda grimaced. "Randi, Horace and I've been talking about one thing that you need to stop doing."

"Oh?"

"Now listen to me. I'm old enough to be your mother. I love you and Steele and those precious children as though you were my very own."

Randi smiled. "I know that, and we love you and Horace."

"Well then, having said that, I need to say something to you that just may be hard for you to hear."

Randi wrinkled her brow. "What, Almeda? What do you need to tell me?"

Almeda drew in a deep breath. "Randi, I know that you love Steele, but quite frankly, you're a flirt."

A surprised look crossed Randi's face. She put her hands to her chest. "What? Almeda, I don't flirt."

Almeda once again reached across the table and took Randi's hands in her own. "Listen to me. You are a flirt."

"How can you say that to me? I don't flirt."

Almeda squeezed Randi's hands. "Yes, you do. I've observed you myself. In social situations you touch men in a flirtatious manner and you flash your eyes at them."

"No, I don't. I'm just making conversation. I like to compliment men, but I compliment women as well. I like to make people feel good about themselves."

Almeda began shaking her head. "Child, listen to me. It's not what you say, it's how you say it."

"I can't believe you're saying these things to me. I'm a friendly person. I'm just being friendly."

Almeda sat staring at Randi. Randi stared back. After a long silence, Almeda leaned toward Randi. "I told you this would not be easy for you to hear. It's not just me, Randi. Other ladies in the parish have asked me to talk to you about this very thing. They are offended when you monopolize their husbands at social events. They don't understand why you always have to wander off. Why don't you stay with your own husband at social affairs?"

Randi dropped her head and began tearing at the tissue in her hand once again. Neither woman spoke. "Randi, I don't want this conversation to put a strain on our friendship, but I really believe you need to listen to me. It's for your own good. But more, it's for Steele as well. I don't know if he's offended by your behavior. He's never said anything to Horace about it. But Randi, your flirtatious nature could end up hurting his ministry. It could even be used against him. His enemies could use it to destroy him and his career."

"I just don't see anything wrong with what I'm doing."

"Randi, how many women do you see kissing Steele on the lips at social occasions?"

Randi shrugged.

"How many married women do you see kissing other women's husbands at social occasions?"

"I've seen you kiss Steele."

"A peck on the cheek from an old woman can hardly be compared to a sexy, young thing like you throwing your arms around a man's neck and kissing him on the lips."

"If that's so offensive, why has no one said anything to me about it until now?"

"I'm amazed that Steele hasn't complained to you about it. He must really love you to put up with that kind of behavior. I don't know of many men who would."

"He's never really said anything. He's told me I'm a flirt, but so is he."

"How many women have you seen Steele grab and kiss on the lips?"

Randi shrugged her shoulders again. "None."

"Exactly. And how would you feel if he did?"

Randi didn't reply.

"It would hurt, wouldn't it? And what else would it lead you to wonder?"

"I guess I'd begin to doubt his love for me."

"And…"

"And what?"

"And what else would you begin to think about?"

"I guess I would begin to wonder if he does that in front of me what is he doing behind my back?"

Almeda smiled and nodded.

"Are you telling me that's what going on with Steele? Do you think he's having those thoughts about me?"

Almeda studied Randi for a few minutes. "What I think isn't important. I think you need to find out what Steele is thinking. If you have done anything or been a part of anything that could be misinterpreted, no matter how innocent you thought at the time, you need to talk to Steele about it."

"I can't think of anything."

"Randi, things can get misinterpreted. Think back to when Steele started acting this way. Then see if you can't recall an incident that you brushed off, but if your husband was told about it, he might conclude otherwise."

Randi shook her head. "I just don't know what it could be." They both sat in silence. Then Randi asked Almeda for the reassurance that she desperately needed. "You said that Steele loves me. You don't doubt that?"

"And I don't doubt it, but child I want you to listen to me right now and you listen to me good. You can kill love. Horace and I both think that you're in danger of killing the love that a really good man has for you. You're in dangerous territory. You have a man that worships you. That's a treasure you don't want to take for granted."

"So you think that's what is bothering Steele?"

"I don't know. It's just something that Horace and I both think you needed to hear. For now, I really think the main problem is the latest round of attacks that group of hypocrites has launched against him."

Randi looked at her watch. "I need to go relieve the sitter. She has a hair appointment."

Almeda walked Randi to her car. She hugged her. "I don't want this conversation to change the way you feel about us. I will never bring it up again. But believe me, Randi; I know what it is to be in an unhappy marriage. You have a good marriage. Nourish it and protect it. I don't care what the optimists have to say. Once it's destroyed, it will never again be the same. And if it is destroyed, I don't believe for a minute you can build a better one once the damage has been done."

Randi nodded and closed the car door.

Chapter 14

THE ONLY THING missing at the annual meeting of the First Church congregation was the sound of a train whistle. Ned Boone and the Idles were manipulating the entire meeting behind the scenes. For the weeks immediately prior to the meeting there had been several neighborhood cottage gatherings. Only those who could be swayed to their way of thinking about Steele Austin were included. Present at the meetings were those that seldom attended First Church but maintained their membership for the three B's – baptizing the babies, binding the matrimonial bonds and burying the bodies.

Steele stood in the back of the packed parish hall with Stone. "I don't think I've ever laid eyes on half the people in this room, Stone."

Stone Clemons clinched his jaw. "They've done their homework. I knew about the cottage meetings. As we were coming in, Almeda told me that they'd also organized a phone bank to call anyone in the parish that they thought they could sway."

"Stone, I may not have the parish membership rolls completely memorized, but there are people here that I'm pretty darn sure aren't even members of this parish."

Stone nodded. "I'd already drawn that conclusion."

"But they're voting."

He nodded again. "I guess we're going to have to start bringing the membership rolls to the meeting and only give ballots to the folks that are recorded on it."

"Well, that doesn't do much to help us tonight."

Stone looked at Steele. "Face it, Father. That group has outsmarted us this year, but I'm going to make sure they don't do it again."

"Looks like Elmer Idle is a sure bet for Senior Warden."

"That's why all these people are here."

"I don't know what I'm going to do with him. I don't look forward to another year with a Senior Warden second guessing my every move."

Stone stood silent looking out over the packed parish hall. "I'll tell you what I think you need to do. Tomorrow morning you bring Elmer in to your office and you lay down the law with him. You set some boundaries and let him know just what you expect from him. Be just as firm as to what you won't tolerate. It's the only way to handle a little snake like him."

"Thanks for the advice. I think I'll do that very thing. It's time for me to give my report." Steele walked to the podium at the front of the hall. He gave his report to the congregation, reciting the number of baptisms, confirmations, weddings, and funerals. He listed the current membership and attendance statistics. He reported on the program and outreach ministries that the parish had initiated the past year. He thanked his staff and the Vestry for their leadership. He thanked Horace Drummond for his ministry and once again welcomed Ginnifer Graystone to the staff. He concluded by thanking the members of the congregation for their ministries. The gathered congregation responded with a polite but less than enthusiastic round of applause. Steele started to leave the podium when he was surprised to hear Ned Boone's voice boom out. "Misturh Austin, I have several questions for you."

Steele felt his legs grow weak. He looked directly at Ned Boone. As expected, he was wearing a bow tie that only accentuated his enlarged Adam's apple. Steele thought his suit would have been quite fashionable during the Great Depression. "Yes, Mister Boone. Please ask your question."

"As I said, I have several questions.

"Go on."

"First, I've been doing an analysis of the parish membership rolls over the past decade. I noticed that on the first annual report after your arrival, this parish lost over two hundred members. This leads many of us to conclude that a significant portion of this congregation responded negatively to your employment as Rector of this great parish."

His comment was followed by several nods and murmurs of agreement. Steele smiled, "You are correct to assume that I am responsible for the loss of membership after my first few months at First Church."

"So you agree that a significant portion of this congregation rejected your call by leaving First Church."

An even bigger smile crossed Steele's face. "No, Mister Boone, if you had taken a closer look at the annual report you would have seen that the loss of membership was due to members being placed on the inactive list or being removed from the rolls."

"I repeat. These people asked to be placed on the inactive rolls or have their membership in First Church revoked because of you!"

"Yes, I am the reason, but the people placed on the inactive rolls and those removed from membership did not request that action. When I arrived, I asked the administrative staff to telephone every person on the parish books that had no record of giving or no record of participation. In the process, we discovered these two hundred people. Many of them had moved to other cities or indicated they had not considered themselves members of this parish for several years. We even discovered a few that had died." Steele's answer was met with a few chuckles.

"I was simply doing what most every new Rector does when he arrives at a parish. I was trying to get an accurate count of my sheep. Remember, the Good Shepherd in the Gospel story only knew that one of his sheep was missing by counting them." His supporters met Steele's answer with a more enthusiastic round of applause.

A disgruntled look washed over Ned Boone's face. "Well, that may be, but we have no way of knowing just how many of those that asked to be removed did so because of you."

Steele chose not to respond. "You said you have several questions."

"It may surprise you to know that I've also done an analysis of our attendance. Of course, we all recognize that attendance numbers are subjective and completely under your control. Several of us have suspected that you've been inflating the attendance numbers for some time. That being said, could you please explain just how it is that we've enjoyed an increase every year you've been Rector except for this past year? You yourself report that our attendance leveled and showed no increase at all this past year."

Again, Steele smiled. "Thank you for asking that question, Mister Boone."

Ned shot Steele a confused look. "Why on earth would you thank me for pointing out that the number of people coming to listen to your sermons has leveled off and is most likely starting to decline?"

"Mister Boone, I hope that you are wrong about one thing."

Ned Boone interrupted, "Misturh Austin, I would advise you not to question my numbers. These are not my numbers. I'm using your numbers as recorded in the attendance record."

Steele took a deep breath. "Mister Boone, I don't dispute your numbers. I was simply suggesting that I hope you are wrong about the impact my preaching has or does not have on attendance. It is my fervent prayer that the primary reason our members come to church is to worship the Almighty and not to hear my sermon."

"You, sir, are wrong about that. We have seen the impact that a good preacher can have on attendance. Your sermons, sir, are formulaic. They do not meet the spiritual needs of many of us in this community." His comment was immediately followed with sporadic applause.

Steele felt his face grow red with embarrassment. "Let's return to your numbers. First, I do not record the attendance numbers. The ushers count the number of worshippers present so that we can prepare the appropriate amount of bread and wine for communion. The attendance slip is given to the Vergers. The Vergers supervise the preparation of the altar. The Verger records the attendance in the register. I do not."

Ned shook his head in disagreement.

"Now as for the leveling of our attendance this past year. Mister Boone, this is a matter of space. When I arrived at First Church, you had two services on Sunday. You had an early service and one large choral service. Since my arrival, we've added an additional choral service in the church and two services in the chapel. We now have five services on Sunday. The addition of each new service has increased the total number of people in worship. We have leveled this past year because every one of these services is now comfortably full. We have also leveled because our priests are stretched about as thin as I dare stretch them. We've added Mother Graystone to the staff so this will make it possible to add another service. The issue is where we are going to have it. The greater issue is that eventually we may need to increase the seating capacity in both the chapel and the church."

"Never!" Ned Boone yelled. "You, sir, will never touch one brick in the church or the chapel. I'll have the Historic Preservation Society all over you. Our sacred buildings have a long and rich history. This congregation will never allow you to change so much as a light fixture." This time the applause was a bit more enthusiastic.

Steele felt himself growing so very tired. He just wanted to end this duel and go home. He was exhausted. He was weary of this combat. He really didn't even want to respond, but he knew he had to say something. "Let's not get ahead of ourselves. I've not organized a building committee or anything that even resembles one. I was simply trying to explain to you why I think our attendance leveled this past year. I don't project much of an increase until such time that we can add another service to accommodate the worshippers."

Ned Boone was energized by the verbal exchange. He could also see that he was wearing Steele Austin down. He was floating on air. He was not about to stop. "Mister Austin, has it ever crossed your mind that First Church is big enough? In fact, some of us think that it's gotten too big." Again, there was some light applause.

Steele felt the wind going out of his sails. He prayed for the energy he needed to respond. "Mister Boone, I'm confused."

A smile of amusement crossed Ned Boone's face. "On that, sir, we do agree. Many of us think that you are confused about a great many things, but we don't have time to get into all that." Steele looked out over the hall to see that several people were nodding. Some were even laughing in agreement.

Steele was tempted to simply walk off the platform and exit the building. "As you like, Mister Boone. Here's my current confusion. You've critiqued the decline in membership after my first year and the current leveling of attendance as signs that the parish is shrinking under my leadership. You have made it known quite often that my leadership style is driving people out of First Church. If you want the parish to continue to decline as you project, I would think that you would be one of my most avid supporters." A roar of laughter echoed around the hall. The loudest round of applause of the evening followed. When the applause and laughter had subsided, Steele looked for Ned Boone. He had resumed his seat. Steele walked off the platform and to the back of the hall. Several people stood to shake his hand as he walked past their tables. There were several comments encouraging him to *hang in there.*

The last item of business was to announce the results of the election. As predicted, Elmer Idle was elected Senior Warden. To Steele's shock, Gary Hendricks was elected Junior Warden. Gary was a past Chairman of the School Board. He was an attorney by profession, with a no-nonsense reputation. Steele could not tell if he supported his ministry or not. He had concluded that he was probably neutral. The one thing that bothered him was that he had been an advocate for separating the school from the parish when he was Chair of the Board. Four new Vestry members were also elected. All four of them were the sons of long time members in the parish that had been openly critical of Steele. He knew now that the tracks were well greased. His immediate task would be to avoid standing in front of the charging locomotive.

Chapter 15

"I BELIEVE YOUR hunch was right, Mrs. Mudd."

Virginia felt herself relax into the leather sofa in Peter McKnight's office. Peter had earned the reputation of being the meanest divorce lawyer in South Georgia. Virginia was well aware of what she thought Henry had on her. What she didn't know for sure was if he knew everything. She was praying that he didn't. She had told Peter McKnight that she'd had an affair, but she didn't tell him with whom. She told him that it really didn't matter since the man didn't live in Falls City anymore and that she really didn't know where he'd moved. She wasn't even sure if she knew his real name and she didn't recall his last name. "It was a very brief thing. I think you could safely call it a one-night stand. It was a stupid mistake, but certainly not a big enough ordeal to destroy our marriage and family." Henry had discovered the affair just days after she'd told the man she never wanted to see him again. She didn't tell him about the abortion. Her story was that Henry had become paranoid because of the affair and had accused her of being pregnant. She assured her attorney that she was not. She had further defined her defense by lying to her attorney and assuring him that one time had been her only indiscretion in the marriage. She had only given in to the man's flirtations because she was so angry with Henry for not being more generous with his money. She had resisted the man's advances, but he still took advantage of her. She wasn't so sure but that he actually had raped her. She put up a fight but finally gave in because he had gotten her so drunk she couldn't fight him off. Other than that one moment of weakness she had been the model wife and mother.

She just didn't understand why Henry couldn't forgive her that single act of stupidity.

"What made you suspect that Henry may have been involved with another woman?"

Virginia searched for a story. Then from somewhere in her twisted mind came what she thought was a most plausible possibility. "Well, I haven't wanted to say anything because I didn't want it to sound like an excuse."

"Go on."

"Well, Mister McKnight, it's like this. I've suspected for sometime that Henry was a player. I even suspected that he'd been in touch with an old girlfriend on a regular basis, but I never really brought it up to him. But it hurt me to think that he was having sex with other women. I'm sure you can understand just what that does to the trust you've placed in your husband. It eventually got to where I just didn't know whether to believe him or not. His infidelity changed the way I felt about him. But worse, it changed the way I felt about myself."

"I'm quite sure that was difficult for you." Peter McKnight was rapidly writing on a yellow legal pad. "Please continue. It's important that you be able to have as accurate a recollection of your feelings as possible."

Virginia put her hand to her breast in an attempt to suggest embarrassment to her attorney. "Yes, of course it is. Well, as I said, I became quite suspicious of Henry just a few years ago. I started going through his things. From time to time I'd find a slip of paper with a telephone number but no name on it in his pocket. I thought that suspicious."

"Did you call the numbers?"

"As a matter of fact I did. On several occasions I would call the number from a pay telephone. I didn't want anyone to be able to trace the number back to our home. Well, every time a woman would answer."

"And?"

Virginia tried to look distraught. "I'd hang up, that's what I'd do."

"You didn't inquire as to who the number belonged to or ask why your husband had the number in his pocket?"

"No…I didn't. I probably should have, but Mister McKnight, you just have to understand how terribly painful this all was for me. I had so many sleepless nights wondering just who my husband was seeing."

Peter McKnight threw his pen down on his desk. "Mrs. Mudd, can I be honest with you?"

"Oh, please do."

"I've been listening to stories of cheating husbands for over twenty years. Stories not unlike your own. And I have to tell you, every time I hear another story it just makes my blood boil. I know that Henry is a fellow member of the Bar and all that, but I promise you I'm going to nail his hide to the courtroom door. We're not going to let him get by with hurting you like he has."

Once again Virginia placed her hand over her heart. She took a tissue and dabbed at her eyes with it. "Oh, Mister McKnight, I just wish that all of this had never happened. I tried to be a good wife and mother. I gave Henry the best years of my life. But it just got to where I couldn't take it anymore."

"And that's why you had the affair?"

"Oh, I know that it was a stupid thing to do. I knew at the time I was doing wrong. Mister McKnight, I'm a Christian woman. I've been active in my church all my life. I could never see myself as an adultereress." Virginia paused and wiped at her eyes with the tissue. "It's just that when you feel like your husband no longer loves you and then an attractive young man gives you a little attention…" Virginia leaned forward on the sofa and blurted, "Mister McKnight, I'm only human. I needed someone to tell me how beautiful I am. I hurt to have a man hold me and give me some affection. I know it was wrong. I admit that, but surely the judge will understand why I did it."

Peter McKnight leaned back in his chair and studied Virginia for a few minutes. "It depends on the Judge. It might surprise you to know that if we draw Judge White we don't have a prayer. Even though she's a woman, she's the worst kind of Baptist. She will not excuse adultery under any circumstances. She's especially hard on unfaithful wives."

"Well, what can we do to make sure we don't get her?"

"I've been thinking about your case. I'd prefer we not go all the way to a trial. I'd like to see if we can't come to an agreement with

Henry. Then we'll simply file the mutual agreement with the court and the decree will be granted. That way we don't get any judge involved in the details. "

"Do you think you can get Henry to agree to that?"

"I think when we hit him with all that we have on him, it's not going to be a problem."

"You mean my suspicions?"

"Oh, I'm going to have your suspicions written up for his attorney, but I've failed to show you what my detectives discovered."

"Oh?"

Peter McKnight smiled. "I suspected infidelity as soon as you told me Henry had served you with divorce papers. I couldn't imagine why a fine upstanding citizen like Henry would divorce such a beautiful woman as yourself. And then to top it all off, why would he want to take your two precious daughters through such a public and potentially messy divorce? No, it just didn't add up. The only reason that a man in Henry's position would file for a divorce would be so that he could be with someone else. So I had my detectives follow him for a few days. We discovered that every day or so he would go to one of those mailing stations where you can rent mailboxes. We discovered he had a mailbox there. He would retrieve a letter, sometimes a couple of them. But the interesting thing was that he would also leave a letter in the mailbox."

"Really?"

Peter McKnight smiled. "Well, I began to question just why a man that has mail delivered to both his home and his office would need a mailbox in a postal annex. But he wasn't using it as a mailbox; he was using it as a drop box. So we decided to watch the mailbox. Within hours we saw this woman…" Peter handed Virginia a picture of a very attractive young woman getting into a car. "Do you recognize her?"

Virginia studied the picture. "No, I've never seen her before."

"Well, it seems she's a receptionist at the hospital. We found out that for a brief time she was a receptionist in your husband's office. She's also going to night school studying to be a paralegal."

"And you think that Henry is involved with this woman?"

Peter leaned back in his chair and laughed. "Mrs. Mudd, I don't think it. I know it."

"How can you know such a thing?"

"Well, we followed her to the hospital. She took the letter that Henry had left in the box and read it at her desk. She then put the letter in her desk drawer. When she went to lunch one of my detectives retrieved the letter."

"And you have it?"

"Not the original. He found several love letters from Henry to this Dee in her drawer. He quickly took pictures of each of them. We have photocopies right here. Do you want to read them?"

Virginia's face dropped. This time real tears did spring to her eyes and roll down her cheeks. "Are you telling me that my Henry really is in love with another woman?"

An inquisitive look appeared on Peter's face. "I thought you told me that you'd suspected such?"

"Oh, I did." Virginia replied quickly. "I guess it's just having it all confirmed is the painful part."

"I know. This all has to be just dreadfully difficult for you. I don't have to tell you the number of women that have sat on that sofa and poured their grief out to me about their cheating husbands. But what I do want to tell you is that I've been able to nail every one of them. I've made every one of the cheating jerks pay, and they've had to pay plenty. Henry Mudd is not going to be my first exception!"

"So you think that if you show him these letters and that picture, you can get him to accept our terms?"

"Oh, I think he'll accept our terms and then some."

"Do you have any pictures of them together?"

"Not yet, but then that's just a matter of time. We're following both of them. We'll get some photos and hopefully some videos."

For the first time in months Virginia not only felt relief, but she felt a small sense of joy. She had leveled the playing field with Henry Mudd. She believed for the first time that she just might be able to keep all her indiscretions secret. She'd make a deal with him. If he didn't tell anyone about hers, she would keep his confidence as well. A smile of satisfaction crept across her face.

"Now, let's continue to build your case. Did Henry travel very much during your marriage?"

"He was gone quite frequently. He would have to take at least one trip every couple of weeks or so."

"And did you ever smell another woman's perfume on his clothes when he returned? Or, perhaps you would find lipstick on his clothing?"

The wheels in Virginia Mudd's head began turning. Soon a story better suited for a daytime soap opera flowed from her lips. Peter McKnight struggled to keep up as he wrote down every word.

Chapter 16

"A COUPLE OF my members that work for you over there at First Church tell me you had another parish meeting filled with contention."

Steele continued to button his cassock. He nodded to Josiah. "You heard right. It's really beginning to wear me down. There's been a group after my hide even before I walked onto the premises."

The Reverend Josiah Williams let out a big baritone laugh. "Well, all is not lost. Seems to me you've been able to win quite a few over. "

"Honestly, brother. I think I have the support of ninety-five percent of the congregation. My antagonists are really just a handful of people. But they're relentless. It's as though I am their full time job. They don't have anything else to do but critique me and my ministry."

"Well, you may be right about that. I read in one of my ministerial journals the other day that most church conflict is started by as few as three or four agitators."

"I count six over at First Church." Steele kissed the cross on the top of his white stole and put it around his neck.

Josiah put his hand on Steele's shoulder. "You know, Steele, it seems to me that some of your white folk just have more time and money on their hands than they know what to do with, so they use it to go after their preacher."

"I think you've got that one right."

"There is something I don't get."

"What's that?"

"Maybe it's because my membership is made up of folks that just don't have a lot of extra money. And as for time, some of them have to work two or even three jobs just to make ends meet. But Steele, they don't come over here to the church to fight with each other or me. They come over here to worship and get some strength and hope to continue to struggle on."

"I've noticed that about your congregation in particular. They really seem devoted to one another. And they appear to this outsider to try to take care of each other."

Josiah nodded. "And as for me, they need me to be in good spirit. They depend on me to nurture their souls and to pastor them when they're down, sick or dying. They know I can't do that if I am all beat up and tired. Do you know that every year they have a *Pastor Appreciation Sunday* on the day that I began my ministry with them? They know that a little appreciation goes a long way."

Steele smiled. "Again, you got that right. I've always thought that it takes at least ten *atta boys* to make up for every *you jerk*."

Once again Josiah let out a roar of laughter. "Rubidoux and I were saying last night that it's a wonderful thing that you and I can do this funeral for Grace together. And it's a good thing we've been able to work on some community projects as well. But I have to be honest with you, Steele. I don't think I want any of your white folk coming over here and joining my church. I've got a peace loving family of black people. Just don't think I want any of your people coming over here and teaching them how to fight with one another."

The two men once again let the laughter roll out of them. "Josiah, I want to thank you for understanding that I really don't want to preach at this funeral. You were Grace's pastor and you're a fantastic preacher. I don't need to say anything."

"I understand, but you're still going to read the tribute, aren't you?"

"I've got it right here. But I have to tell you that this tribute goes on longer than most of my sermons."

"That's something else I don't get. Most of you white preachers are just warming up when you quit preaching."

Steele smiled, "That's because our congregations, for the most part, won't sit for a sermon that goes longer than fifteen or twenty minutes."

Josiah shook his head. "Now that's just sad. You're not giving them bad news. You're preaching the Good News. You're giving them the most important message they'll ever hear in their lives. How can you put a time limit on God? I just don't get it."

Just then a man in a black suit with a white carnation in the lapel walked in. "Reverend Williams, the body has arrived and the family has been seated. We're ready to begin."

Steele and Josiah walked through the door from his office directly onto the platform in the front of the church. As Steele remembered, there was an organist, a pianist, several guitarists, some brass instrumentalists, and a large set of drums. The choir was seated behind the ministers' seats. The organist and pianist were building the volume of their prelude. When Steele and Josiah entered, the choir and congregation stood. The other instrumentalist immediately joined the prelude.

The choir began to sway and clap their hands. Soon several in the congregation were doing so as well. Josiah walked up to the pulpit, and in a loud voice proclaimed, "*I am the resurrection and the life saith the Lord. So why do you seek the living among the dead? If you are look-*ing for our sister, Grace, she is not here! She's gone home. She's gone home. She's gone home to be with Jesus.

Some men ask, how are the dead to be raised? With what kind of body will they be born? We have Grace's body here, but Grace is not here. Alleluia. Alleluia. *That which we sow is physical. That which will be raised is spiritual. For all die, but in Christ all will be made alive.*"

Steele did not think it was possible for the music to get any louder, but it did. Then Josiah waved his hand and immediately the music became barely audible. Josiah leaned over the pulpit. "Now listen to me my children. *Jesus said that he was going to prepare a place for us and that he would come again and receive us unto Himself. He said I know my sheep and my sheep know me. I call them each by name.*" Then Josiah shouted, "Grace, Grace, the Lord is calling your name. Grace is not here. She's gone home to be with Jesus." The music immediately became almost deafening as the choir and people stood and shouted *Alleluia! Alleluia!*

"If you believe in Jesus then you know that whoever lives in Jesus will never die. She is not here!" Then he got progressively louder. "She is not here! She is not here!" More shouts of *Amen* and *Hallelujah* rose up from the congregation. Then the choir started singing.

Goose pimples spread over Steele's arms as the fervor of the worship continued to increase. He looked out at the congregation. He spotted Chief Sparks and his wife. He saw that Stone was sitting with Horace and Almeda. Several of the staff members from First Church that had known Willie were there. But what struck him the most was the number of white uniformed police officers present. It was as though the entire police force had come to show their respect for Grace and Willie's grandsons.

Grace's two grandsons read the scripture readings. A long prayer was offered by one of the leading members of the congregation. The choir offered several moving anthems. Then it was Steele's turn to read the tribute. He reminded the congregation that Grace was the grand-daughter of a slave. She was always grateful that her mother's family was kept together, even though the common practice at the time was to divide families and sell the children off separately. He reminded them that she married Willie at an early age. They had one daughter that had been killed in a car accident. She and Willie had raised her twin sons. She worked as a domestic all her life to help support the family and to insure that her grandsons could have every opportunity. Grace loved telling the story of the first time she and Willie were able to vote for a President of the United States. She had worked hard in the NAACP, the Service League of the Church, and the Women's Auxiliary. She and Willie had also led the youth Bible Study in the parish for close to fifty years. Her two grandsons, who are officers in the Falls City Police Department, their wives, two great grandchildren, her entire church family and a large company of friends survive her. Her parents, her only daughter, and her husband preceded her in death. She now joins them in heaven where there is much rejoicing at her arrival. When Steele had finished reading the tribute, he took his seat next to Josiah. The choir stood and sang one of the most stirring renditions of *I Want to Ride That Glory Train* he had ever heard in his life. By the time the choir had finished, everyone in the church was on their feet clapping or waving their hands in the air. Steele was beginning to feel his own soul renewed by the worship in the room.

Josiah chose to preach on the thirty-first chapter of Proverbs, the tenth verse. *Who can find a virtuous woman? For her price is far above rubies. The heart of her husband doth safely trust in her, so that he shall have no need of spoil. She will do him good and not evil all the days of her life.*

Josiah proclaimed that these words were an accurate description of Grace. From the moment she fell in love with Willie, she had no use for any other man. Willie was the love of her life. He was her soul mate. Just as God created Eve from the rib of Adam, so He created Grace from the rib of Willie. The two of them were inseparable. Those who knew them never spoke of the one without the other. It was always Willie and Grace. If you saw Willie you knew that Grace was nearby. And if you saw Grace you knew that Willie would be somewhere close, looking at her like a lovesick schoolboy. More precious than rubies or a jewel of any price is a faithful wife in whom a husband can put his complete trust. Grace never did anything in her entire life to hurt Willie. She only brought goodness into their marriage.

As Steele listened to Josiah, the photo of his own wife with her hands on the man's naked chest flashed before his eyes. Until he had seen those pictures, he had believed that he was one of the lucky men in life that had married a jewel beyond price. He thought he'd married a real lady. Beyond that, he'd believed that Randi was so devoted to him and their children that she'd never do anything to hurt any of them. Now he just didn't know. He needed that detective to find out for sure. But if she were being unfaithful to him, that meant he would have to decide whether or not to divorce her. He knew that he could never again feel the same way about her. If it was true, he knew that a part of him would die. The pictures had already shrunk a portion of his soul. He knew that his love for Randi had already been changed. It was like a death. He knew he was grieving already for what he thought they had together. He was grieving for the love that he'd felt for her. His biggest decision would be putting Travis and Amanda through the trauma of divorce. He just didn't know if he could do that. He felt someone pull on his arm. "It's time to go stand by the remains, Father Austin." Steele nodded at the funeral director. Josiah was already standing at the head of the open casket. The worshippers were starting to file past to bid their final farewells.

The procession to the First Church Cemetery was quite a sight. Each of Grace's grandsons was driving police cruisers with flashing lights in front and on either side of the hearse. Their wives and children rode with them. Motorcycle officers blocked all the side streets. The road to the cemetery was devoid of any traffic. There were at least another dozen police cruisers in the procession filled with Falls City officers and their families. It was less than a mile to First Church but it took nearly an hour for all the vehicles to arrive. The cemetery was filled with people. When they arrived at the open grave, Josiah and Steele stood quietly until all the mourners could arrive. The mix of people at the cemetery was a replica of the congregation gathered in the church. Josiah was the first to make the observation. He whispered, "Look out there, Steele. I believe there's just about as many white folks as there are black ones."

Steele nodded.

"We've come a long way since we buried Willie here."

Again, Steele nodded. "Yes, we have. But Josiah, my friend, we have so far to go."

"Are you going to stay here at First Church and go the rest of the way with me?"

Steele felt his eyes cloud with tears. "I don't know if it's going to be my decision."

Josiah patted Steele on the back. "I think there's more to the story then you're telling me. I'm here if you want to talk."

It was all Steele could do to maintain his composure. He felt his lips begin to quiver. As he walked away from the grave he felt like his legs were made of lead. Several people reached out to shake his hand. Some wanted to make polite conversation, but Steele really just wanted to get to his office. He thought about stopping by the chapel to have some quiet time and say some prayers but decided against it. He just needed a place to hide, but where?

Chapter 17

STEELE WALKED INTO Crystal's office. "Are there any messages?"

"Nothing that can't wait until tomorrow. You've already had a long day, but there are some priests waiting to see you."

"Did I have an appointment with them? "

"No, they were here to see Dr. Drummond. They were hoping that you would have just a few minutes for them."

Steele nodded. "Where are they?"

"In the waiting room. Do you want me to show them in to your office?"

"No, I'll go get them."

Steele walked across the hall to the waiting room. There were five priests standing in a circle talking. He recognized all of them. "Hey guys, this is a surprise. Come to my office. Can I get you anything to drink? Coffee? Sodas?"

The group followed Steele into his office. "No, we won't take long. We just need to talk with you about a very urgent matter."

Steele invited them all to sit down. "Okay, what can I do for you?"

One of the clergy pointed to the senior cleric in the group. "Lynn here will do our talking for us."

Steele smiled at Lynn. He knew him through the Diocese and at the various gatherings of the clergy. He was the Rector of a medium sized parish in Savannah. "Okay, Lynn. What can I do for you?"

"Well, Steele, as you know, Rufus Peterson has called for the election of a successor. He plans to retire as soon as one is elected."

"Yes, I received his letter. I know that his health continues to be an issue for him, but more than that, I think he's just grown tired."

"That may be, but we need to get the right man nominated, and if possible, elected."

"What does that have to do with me?"

"Well, Steele, we need your permission…"

Steele interrupted, "Lynn, let me stop you right there. I don't want to be the Bishop of this Diocese. Quite frankly, I think I am far too young. My personal bias is that we shouldn't elect anyone to that office who is younger than fifty-five."

"Oh, we agree with you on that." Lynn looked at the other clergy he was representing. "We don't want you to get the wrong impression, but we didn't come to ask if we could nominate you, although we all agree that you'd make a fine Bishop."

Steele wrinkled his brow. "Then what is it you do need to ask me?"

"We want you to give us permission to nominate Horace Drummond."

Steele relaxed into his wing back chair. "Have you talked to Horace about this?"

"We have, but he says that he won't do it unless he has your blessing."

"Of course. I'll give him my blessing. I would never stand in Horace's way if he feels called to that office. He'll have my complete support."

"That's wonderful news. Thank you so much."

"Let's call Horace down here. I want him to know that I will be his greatest supporter." Steele walked over to the intercom and punched the numbers to Horace's office. When Horace answered, Steele joked, "Bishop Drummond, this is one of your humble servants. Will you please come down to my office?"

"Are you going to take me out behind the woodshed?"

Steele chuckled. "Quite to the contrary. We're inviting you to your campaign headquarters."

When Horace arrived, the others stood and applauded. "Okay, okay." He motioned for everyone to sit down. "I've had some time to think about this and I believe we need to talk some things through. I want to talk them through honestly and with no reservations."

Everyone resumed their seats. "I knew that Steele would give me his blessing, but I just needed to hear him say it. He's just that kind of guy and he's just that kind of friend to me. But Lynn, just in case you haven't noticed, my skin color is not the result of too much South Georgia sun. This won't wash off. I know that there are other African American Bishops, but do you really think that the Diocese of Savannah is ready for a black Bishop?"

"We did our homework before we asked you, Horace. We've talked to over half the clergy in the Diocese. Now granted, we've talked to the clergy that we think will support your nomination. We also think they'll be able to bring their lay delegates along as well. We are not asking you to be our Bishop because you're black. We're asking you to be our Bishop because of you."

Horace smiled. "Well, there is one more problem that just might make it even more difficult for some of the people in this Diocese to swallow. I'm married to a white woman."

Lynn once again looked around the room at the other clergy. "Horace, let me assure you we've thought all that through. We've sent out the trial balloons and that just is not going to be an issue for most of us. I know this is Georgia and we are a conservative people slow to change, but the battle will not be fought over your race or that of your wife."

Horace shrugged. "Well, then tell me about your process. How did you choose me?"

Lynn pulled two sheets of paper out of his coat pocket and handed one to Steele and the other to Horace. "These are the names being brought forth by the nominating committee. I am on the committee. We've had a very difficult time getting suitable candidates. All the Rectors of the big parishes across the country we contacted turned us down. Several were honest enough to tell us that they simply couldn't afford the cut in compensation to be a Bishop. We then went after some of the names that all of us would recognize, but we were equally unsuccessful. Every one of them, to the person, told us they believed they could have a more effective ministry as a Rector of a parish than they could as a Bishop. The names you have before you are the ones that have agreed so far."

Steele gave a low whistle. "You've got two deployment officers, neither of whom have ever been in charge of even a tiny congregation. You've got one fellow here who has never attended an Episcopal Seminary. And the fourth one on your list has run in at least a half dozen Episcopal elections. He definitely has purple in his eyes."

"I fear you've pretty accurately summarized our list."

Steele looked at Horace. "Brother, I want you also to note that every one of them is at least twenty years your junior."

Horace nodded.

"But that's the point." Lynn said eagerly. "The clergy of this Diocese have been so beaten up under Rufus Petersen we don't want to enter another twenty year marriage. Horace here can give us the break we need to recover. He can be Bishop for five years or longer if he wants, but quite frankly, if any one of the guys on this list is elected, most of us will be leaving the Diocese."

"I wouldn't want to do the job for more than five to seven years. I can certainly assure you that I won't want to do it for ten years."

"Steele, don't you see? That's just what we need. We need a man with Horace's integrity and ability to pastor the clergy of this Diocese. Most of us are still nursing open wounds that Rufus Petersen inflicted on us. We need time to heal."

"Where did these deployment officers come from?"

Lynn gave the others a knowing look. "Jim Vernon. He's thrown his complete support behind the first one on the list. Seems they know each other through the Deployment Officers' meetings."

"But he has no parish experience. He's never been in charge of anything."

"We know that, but Canon Vernon has already browbeat a lot of the mission clergy and some of the Rectors of the smaller parishes into supporting this guy. "

Horace handed the sheet of paper back to Lynn. "Canon Vernon is pretty new to the table himself. Didn't you tell me, Steele, that he has no seminary training?"

"I'll answer that if you don't mind, Steele." Lynn's face was growing red. "Not only has he never been to seminary, he's never been in charge of a congregation either. The only thing he has going for him is that he's a complete control freak. He bullies his way into every situation. In some ways he's worse than Rufus Petersen ever thought about being. He's completely untrustworthy."

Steele made the timeout motion with his hands. "Whoa, Lynn. Those are pretty strong words."

"Steele, you've obviously not had to deal with him just yet."

"Oh, but I have."

"And?"

"It wasn't very pleasant."

Lynn pointed to two of the other clergy. "Three of us here have literally had calls to other parishes taken from us because of Canon Vernon. Steele, he's a liar of the worst kind."

"And what kind is that?"

"He's a sneaky liar."

"I had received a call to a parish in another Diocese. Jim Vernon called up the chair of the search committee and told him that he really needed to withdraw the call. He told him that there were some things about me that he just couldn't discuss, but they were serious. He told him that they would be making a tragic mistake if they called me to be their Rector."

"I'm sorry, Lynn. That's just unforgivable."

Lynn continued. "Rufus Petersen has given over all the deployment issues to Friar Mean. That's what the clergy have nicknamed him. If you won't agree to be his stooge, he bad mouths you to Search Committees, Vestries, other Deployment Officers, and even to Bishops."

"Charlie over here was on a list and was about to receive the call to a sizeable congregation. Friar Mean called up the Bishop of that Diocese and told him that they were making a terrible mistake and that they needed to remove him from consideration. Well, the Bishop told him that they'd run all the references on Charlie and that he had glowing recommendations. Jim Vernon told that Bishop they just weren't talking to the right people. He cost Charlie that call. The man is a snake. Horace, we're hoping that one of the first things you'll do is get rid of him when you're elected. No one in this Diocese trusts him. We need you to give us a Bishop's office that we can trust."

Horace nodded.

"But you have to do it for the lay people in this Diocese, not just the clergy. The Canon insists on accompanying the Bishop to all his meetings and visits. That means he has several hours alone in the car with him. That's in addition to all the access he has to the Bishop in his office. By the time poor ol' Peterson gets to a meeting, the Canon has him so worked up that he goes in with both guns blasting. He and the Canon join forces verbally attacking priests, search committees and Vestries, demanding that they do what the Canon wants them to do. He fills the Bishop's head with lies and distortions. They even tell Vestries that if they don't do as the Canon wants them to do there will be repercussions. They tell them they have the right to take complete control of the situation under Canon Law. The clergy are the only ones that can challenge them on that because we know that what they want to do is not lawful. But their methodology is to meet with the Search Committees and Vestries without any clergy present so that they won't be challenged or corrected. Horace, we can't have this pattern repeated with the next Bishop, but it will be if our current Deployment Officer is still in place."

"I understand. But if what you say is true, it sounds like the Canon will work pretty hard against my nomination, let alone my election."

"We already have enough votes on the nominating committee to get you nominated. We just needed your consent. Friar Mean won't be able to do anything about that unless he can dig up some dirt on you."

Horace released a deep laugh. "Now, gentlemen, let me tell you. If you're looking for a candidate that's never ticked off a parishioner or a fellow priest, you need to keep looking. I've even got one Bishop that I worked for that thinks I am the Devil incarnate. God only knows what he might say about me. He's a really disgusting little man. If folks go digging around in my past, they're going to be able to find people that think less of me than I would like. I can think of a couple that would love to get even with me for some imagined wrong they think I did to them."

"And that's the very reason that we can't get some of the best people to even run for Bishop. Friar Mean does not have a corner on deception. There are just too many Christians, including priests and bishops out there, that are short on forgiveness and long on meanness." Steele handed his sheet of paper back to Lynn. "Horace, have you discussed all this with Almeda?"

Horace winked at Lynn. "Oh, I was hoping you'd do that for me."

"I don't think so. I love you like a brother, but that's a job you're going to have to do yourself."

Horace nodded and smiled. "Guess you're right. Never send a boy to do a man's job."

"I'm not sure that one man is enough. You may want to take this committee with you." Steele shot back.

"We'll see. We'll see. I can just see Almeda now. You know for certain she's going to be one of those Bishop's wives that wears purple and a big gold cross."

Steele looked back at the committee. "I now understand. Our biggest obstacle in this is not Horace's skin color or his marriage to Almeda. It's going to be the Canon of Mean."

Lynn nodded. "We are all putting our ministries at risk by going up against him, but it's just something we have to do. I don't think we have a choice."

Steele looked over at Horace. "Bishop Drummond. I like the sound of that. Will you now give us your blessing?"

Horace stood. When he did Steele and the other priests knelt on the floor to receive his blessing.

Chapter 18

"STEELE, I INSIST!" Randi was not to be dissuaded. "Travis really misses you. He's been looking forward to going to the park and zoo with you. I've already made arrangements with Crystal to clear your calendar. No one is going to disturb you. And I want you to take Amanda as well."

"Oh, and what do you plan to do?" Steele tried not to sound suspicious.

"Steele, I just want some time alone. I may take a nap, read a book, or just sit and stare. I don't know. I've been with the children constantly for the past few weeks. I need a break and these babies need some time with their father. Now go, and don't come back before five o'clock. If you do, I'll have all the doors locked and I won't let you in."

"Well, that does sound suspicious."

"Steele, please. Go and have a nice afternoon with your children. Travis is so excited. I've got Amanda's diaper bag all packed for you and her stroller is waiting at the door. She'll probably nap most of the time you're gone, but the fresh air will be good for her."

"But before you go, Steele Austin, it's time that you give me some honest answers!" Randi had that very familiar determined tone in her voice. Steele had dealt with it before and he knew there would be no avoiding her.

"Randi, do we have to do this right now? I'm just so tired."

"Steele, you've not touched me in weeks. You almost have to force yourself even to peck me on the lips. We never talk. You act like you don't want to be around me. I'm entitled to an explanation of just what is going on with you."

Steele pleaded. "Randi, I've told you a dozen times I've just got more on my plate then I can say grace over. I'm exhausted."

"I know that you're under the gun, but I don't think that's all there is to it. You've had a lot of pressure put on you before, but it never came between the two of us. In fact, it brought us closer." The look of determination on Randi's face grew more rigid. "Steele, I don't know what I possibly could have done to make you treat me the way you have. I've apologized over and over again for my unnamed offenses. But that doesn't seem to be enough for you. Now, I want some answers of my own."

Steele stood to leave. "Randi, please let's do this later? Travis and Amanda are waiting on me."

"Sit back down, Steele. Travis is playing next door and the neighbor is watching Amanda. I want some answers and I want them now. Steele Austin, are you having an affair?"

It was as though Randi had thrown a bucket of ice water in Steele's face. He was stunned. He didn't know how to answer her.

"Should I interpret your silence as a yes?"

Steele quickly gathered his thoughts. "No, Randi, absolutely not."

"Well, let me be a little more specific. Are you having extended telephone conversations with another woman on a regular basis?"

"Randi, no."

"Well, then are you sneaking off to have lunch or coffee with another woman on a regular basis?"

"Randi, I can't believe you're asking me these questions. Where is this coming from?"

"Listen here, buddy. That's not an answer. You don't answer a question with a question. Are you seeing another woman on a regular basis?"

"No, Randi. I promise you on a stack of Bibles I am not."

"Have you written love letters or bought gifts for another woman?"

"Randi, you see every penny I earn and you also see where every penny goes."

"Again, not an answer."

"Have your lips been on the lips of another woman?"

Steele wanted to lighten the moment. "Okay, you've got me there. I meant to kiss Almeda on the cheek, but I accidentally brushed her lips."

"Not funny." Randi was now glaring at Steele. "Okay, one last question and I want an honest answer. Believe me, you don't want to lie to me on this one."

"Randi, I've never lied to you and I have no need to do so now."

"Steele Austin, has any part of your body been inside another woman since we got married?"

"Randi, no. There's never been anyone else but you. From the day I met you, I've not been physically intimate with anyone but you."

Randi continued to glare at Steele. He didn't know whether she believed him or not. He was having a difficult time wrapping his mind around her interrogation. He had been suspecting her of doing the very things that she was cross-examining him on. The fact that she knew all the right questions to ask made him even more suspicious. "Are we finished?"

"For now, but Steele Austin, you need to know something. I love you with all my heart, but I can't keep living this way. I don't know what's wrong with you, but I suggest you get it fixed and you do so soon."

"Or?" Steele wrinkled his brow.

Tears welled up in Randi's eyes. "Steele, I just can't." She then ran up the stairs and closed the bedroom door.

Steele went next door and picked up Travis and Amanda so that he could take them to the park. He was going to meet someone there. They would be waiting on him. He didn't tell Randi. He hoped that he would never have to tell her.

Chapter 19

NED BOONE, ELMER Idle and Canon Jim Vernon were meeting for lunch at The Magnolia Club. Ned had arranged for them to have one of the small private dining rooms upstairs so that they wouldn't be disturbed. "I have to admit that I was a bit surprised to hear that you wanted to meet with us, Canon Vernon." Ned Boone's Adam's apple dangled over his bow tie.

"Well, Mister Boone, as Elmer might have told you, we have a great deal in common."

Ned Boone smiled and nodded his agreement.

"I know that you gentlemen have only the best interests of First Church at heart. I want to assure you that is also the case with me and my office in the Diocesan House."

Just then a black waiter wearing black pants, a white shirt, white jacket, and black bow tie entered the room. "Misturh Boone, what's kin I get you and yor' guests?"

"Have you boys decided what you'd like to eat?"

"I think the vegetable plate looks good." Elmer Idle closed his menu. "Bring me the fried okra, the turnip greens, the cheese grits and the fried apples. And bring us another basket of these cornbread sticks."

"That does sound good." Jim Vernon agreed.

"Make it three." Ned nodded. "And bring us a pitcher of sweet tea."

After the waiter had departed and closed the door behind him, Ned sat studying the Canon's face. An uncomfortable silence fell on the table. Ned needed to test the cleric one more time. "Canon Vernon, I need to be frank with you. We are fighting for the very survival of First Church. Steele Austin in on the verge of destroying our beloved parish."

Canon Vernon nodded. "Can I be perfectly candid with you?"

"Please do." Ned frowned.

"As you know, the Bishop and I have been quite concerned about Steele Austin's style of leadership."

"I thought the Bishop had a change of heart on Austin." Elmer questioned. "I was under the impression that he was now president of the Steele Austin Fan Club."

"Oh, quite the contrary." Jim Vernon's voice rose in volume. "The Bishop is not going to tell you this because, quite frankly, he's just grown tired of this entire mess. As you know, he's decided to retire. But I can tell you that he blames Austin for his heart attack. In fact, he told me just the other day that if it weren't for Austin and all the trouble at First Church, he would remain as our Bishop. We can blame the loss of our beloved Bishop on Steele Austin."

A very satisfied look crossed both Ned and Elmer's faces. Ned winked at Elmer. "So you think the Bishop would now work with us to get rid of Austin?"

"I wish I could tell you that he would, but gentlemen, the man is just worn out. We seldom see him in the office. For all practical purposes he's already retired. I can assure you this. He won't be getting in our way."

"So who's running the Diocese?"

"I am."

"That's good to hear." Elmer smiled.

"Canon Vernon, you know that Elmer here is the new Senior Warden?"

"I do. Congratulations on your election. I understand it was a landslide."

"Well, let's just say that we had a lot of people show up for the parish meeting that had all but given up on First Church. But they're back and they've voted for change."

"Elmer, have you met with the Rector?" Ned asked.

"No, he's asked to meet with me, but I've been putting him off. I knew that we would be having this meeting with Canon Vernon. I wanted to see what he had on his mind before meeting with Austin."

Ned made chewing motions with his mouth. "Where is that waiter with our food? I'm telling you, some of them are so damn slow you need a hot poking iron to get them moving." Ned walked to the dining room door and opened it. "Oh, there you are. What took you so long?"

"I'sa sure sorry, Misturh Boone, but the kitchen's all backed up. They hav'n a big party downstairs."

"What kind of party?"

"I think it's some sort of fund raiser."

After they were all served and the door was once again secure, Ned sat straight up in his chair and pointed his finger at Canon Vernon for emphasis. "That's part of the problem right there. Austin has come into our town and started all kinds of liberal, bleeding heart, do-good organizations. I wouldn't be a bit surprised if he isn't the one hosting that party downstairs and with First Church money. He's an absolute disgrace. He doesn't know the first thing about pastoring a church."

"The Bishop and I couldn't agree with you more. The Bishop has told me on more than one occasion that if First Church had given the Diocese the money that Austin has wasted on his liberal causes, he could have done some great things for God in this state."

"Didn't the Diocese partner with Austin on that motel for the queer boys?"

Jim Vernon's lips tightened. "Let's get one thing straight. Austin took advantage of the Bishop. It had just been a few weeks after the Bishop had his heart attack. He was taking some very strong medicine. He was in a vulnerable state. Austin completely manipulated the man. He took advantage of his situation. That's unforgivable."

Elmer was curious. "And the Bishop told you this?"

"Just this very morning, as a matter of fact. He knew I was meeting with you and he wanted me to clear that very matter up."

"So what ideas do you have on how we might proceed?"

Canon Vernon took the last bite of his grits, wiped his mouth with his napkin, and leaned back in his chair. "You realize that one of the nominees for Bishop of this Diocese is going to be Horace Drummond?"

"What?" Both Elmer and Ned shouted at the same time.

"I can't do anything about the nomination. There is a group of clergy supporting him. He has enough votes on the nominating committee to be on the ballot. But just so you'll know, I am digging around in his past. There just might be something back there we can use against him."

"Do you need any help with that?"

"Thanks for asking, Mister Boone, but I think I have all the resources I need."

"If you need some money to hire an investigator, just let me know."

Jim Vernon chuckled. "Oh, I think the gossip wheels in the church are oiled well enough for me to find out anything I need to know. I just have to find one person that Drummond has crossed. They'll lead me to others. Jealousy and envy have been used on more than one occasion against a priest. They are powerful motivators."

"We've got to stop this. We do not want Horace Drummond to be Bishop of this Diocese. We don't even want him at First Church."

Elmer nodded. "And we don't want Austin's latest hire here either. We want to be rid of Austin, Drummond, and his new priestess." Elmer could feel his face growing flush with anger. "My wife is on the staff down there and she tells me that most of the lay staff needs to go as well. They're all so enamored with Austin they can't even see straight. She says most of them don't do a thing. They just sit around, smoke cigarettes, and drink the coffee that we pay for with our tithes."

"When my candidate is elected, he'll solve all the personnel issues at First Church."

"Oh." Ned smiled. "Tell us about your candidate."

"First, you need to know that he's a good friend of mine, so I have complete confidence in him. He's the Canon for Deployment in the Diocese of Mobile, but he's from Georgia, so he's a Georgia boy. He knows our state and he knows our Diocese. I already have his ear and he is in total agreement with me about the state of affairs at First Church. The first thing he'll do is revoke Ginnifer Graystone's license.

She won't be able to pretend to be a priest in this Diocese. He's working with me to see what we can find on both Austin and Drummond. There's just got to be something back there on both of them. They can't be as squeaky clean as they pretend to be."

"I don't know." Ned shook his head. "We've tried everything we know how to do to try to get something on Austin, but so far he's like Teflon. Nothing sticks."

"Have you ever looked into Drummond's background?"

"Not really. I don't guess we ever felt like he was much of a threat."

"Well, if he does become Bishop of this Diocese he'll be much more than a threat. We all know that he's Steele Austin's best friend. We simply can't let that happen."

Ned and Elmer looked at each other and shrugged. "I'm just not sure we know how we can help you. I've never been at a convention to elect a Bishop. Have you, Ned?"

Ned shook his head. "Tell us what you need us to do."

"As I said, we can't stop his nomination. That plane has already been cleared for take off, but we can make sure that he's not elected."

"How?"

"Well, this is where it gets interesting and it's going to require the both of you to become Academy Award winning actors."

"Sounds like fun." Elmer smiled. "Go on."

"Well, we need to start by having the both of you pretend that you're ecstatic over Horace's nomination."

"Oh, I don't know if I'm that good of an actor. I don't know, Ned. Do you think we can pull that off?"

"Sure you can. You just don't make this election about Drummond, you make it about First Church. One of the clergy from First Church is going to be elected a Bishop. That's historic. That would qualify First Church as a *Bishop Maker*. That's a reputation any parish can be proud of. Now can't the two of you support that? I need the two of you to get excited about this. Talk it up in the congregation. Have some parties for Horace to celebrate his nomination. Write articles for the newsletter. Give speeches. I don't care. Just make sure that everyone is completely convinced that you are behind Drummond. But the two people that it is absolutely critical you convince are Austin and Drummond."

Elmer frowned. "Okay, even if we can pull that off, how is that going to keep him from being elected? Sounds to me like we're helping him."

A large smile crossed Jim Vernon's face. "Lean in here boys. I'm going to whisper my plan to you. I'm only going to say this one time. Elmer, you're going to play a pivotal role." The three men all leaned toward the center of the table. When Canon Jim Vernon had revealed his plan, they leaned back in their chairs. Large smiles of satisfaction were on all their faces.

"And you really think that will work?" Ned inquired eagerly.

"If you all do your part, I know it will work."

"Where's that waiter?" Ned Boone exploded. I'm ordering a bottle of champagne. We've finally got something to really celebrate."

Chapter 20

THE WOMEN'S CLUB of Falls City is responsible for one of the most beautiful parks in the entire state. It's located just blocks from the city center. There are several natural and man-made waterfalls in the park. A world famous landscape architect designed the park itself. His only instruction from the ladies was to make an abundant use of the many types of flowers that flourish so easily in South Georgia.

The park was filled with azaleas of all colors. Camellias and gardenias each bloomed majestically in their season. Magnolias, South Georgia pines, and dogwoods were strategically placed throughout the park. Large live oak trees gave shade. There were also several *Memorial Gardens* denoted by large brass plaques. The rose garden was particularly well done, but there was also a flower garden landscaped with perennials and several flower gardens where the annuals were rotated each season.

The Annual Magnolia Ball sponsored by the Women's Club was their primary fundraiser. Anyone who was anyone in Falls City was sure to be in attendance. But so too were the many *social climbers* that were more than willing to lay out a minimum of two hundred and fifty dollars per couple to be in attendance. Of course, if you wanted a reserved table and an invitation to the cocktail party to meet the visiting celebrity, then you could plan on spending up to ten thousand dollars for the opportunity to impress.

The Women's Club of Falls City was a vast organization compared to the Debutante Society, the Cotillion, or even the Junior League. The Club's membership certainly exceeded that of the Daughters of the Confederacy. The membership requirements were a lot less strict since the women needed a much larger membership to support their many charitable endeavors in the city. Most anyone who could afford the annual dues of one hundred dollars per month could join. Of course, people of color, Roman Catholics, and members of the Jewish religion were discouraged.

The stately old mansion that served as the official offices of the Women's Club sat near the entrance to the park. It was a large brick plantation house that had been converted for club purposes. In many ways it mirrored the design of the all male Magnolia Club, with several exceptions. There were private meeting rooms in the club, a large dining room where lunch and dinner were served each day, and an even larger ballroom that was a favorite for wedding receptions. Unlike The Magnolia Club, a bride's family did not have to be members of the Women's Club to utilize the facilities for their wedding festivities. They needed only pay the rental fee charged by the club and utilize the club's catering service. Of course, the board had also made arrangements to receive a *referral fee* from the various florists, limousine services, bridal shops, and even several of the local bands that often played at the receptions.

While the membership was large, the listing of the board members was taken directly from the membership roles of First Church. The income from their various activities gave the board an annual financial statement that more than rivaled any other charitable endeavor in Falls City. Its annual budget far exceeded that of any local church and certainly surpassed that of First Church and First Church School combined. These resources were never wasted. They were returned each year to the people of Falls City. The park named for the Women's Club and the Falls City Zoo were the primary recipients. The end result was a park and zoo that was on the *Must See List* published by the Department of Tourism for the State of Georgia.

Steele and the children arrived at the park. Travis immediately ran for the playground. There was a toy elephant sitting on a large spring. He climbed up on it and began rocking back and forth. Steele took a seat on a bench just a few feet from Travis so that he could watch him. He gave Amanda her bottle and then burped her on his shoulder. Soon she was asleep. He put her back in the stroller and pulled the screen down to protect her from the sun and any menacing insects that might be in the area.

"There you are, Father Austin."

Steele turned toward the voice. He stood to shake the hand of Tim Roberts. "Please, sit down."

"These are my children. This is Amanda. She's having her afternoon siesta. And the fellow over there wearing out that elephant is my son, Travis." Then Steele caught himself. "But then I guess you already knew that."

Tim nodded. "Seems to me this park has the names of your members written all over it."

"I'm afraid you're right. The women of First Church are quite active in community affairs."

"And everything else in this town. I fear that if we ever have a real good rain most of your members will drown."

Steele smiled. "Oh, some of them are awfully pleased with themselves. You're right about that, but they're just like the rest of us once you strip their faux exterior away."

"And that's why you're a priest and I'm a private investigator. I fear I can't be that charitable when it comes to many of the people over there at First Church." Tim turned his head to look behind him at the landscaping on the hillside. "You've found a good place to sit."

"I'm afraid I have to give the credit to Travis. He chose the spot."

Tim took in a deep breath. "Do you smell that? It's the smell of the sweet bay magnolia tree. They just fill the air with their fruity fragrance."

"They do smell good." Steele agreed. He really didn't want to talk about magnolia trees. He wanted to get a report. "Do you have anything for me?"

Tim shook his head and pursed his lips. "Father Austin, what I hope I have for you is good news. We've not found anything."

Steele felt himself relax. "Nothing."

"Honest, Father. I'd love to keep taking your money, but our investigation is simply not turning up anything. We've had a tail on your wife for over two weeks now. She's not doing anything out of the ordinary. Just the usual housewife and mommy stuff. There's absolutely nothing to call to your attention."

Steele took in a deep breath. "What about the wiretap on the telephone?"

"Again, Father Austin, nothing. She chats with her girlfriends. She chats with her mother and your mother, but nothing out of the ordinary. She's quite concerned about you and, quite frankly, she's beginning to worry if your marriage is in trouble. She's blaming herself for a lot of things. She fears that since the birth of Amanda you no longer find her attractive."

Steele sat silently watching Travis, who had now moved from the elephant to a swing.

"Let me ask you, Father Austin, does your wife ever take out of town trips without you? Perhaps she has such a trip planned? Maybe she plans to take a trip with a girlfriend or with a girlfriend that you've never met? Maybe she needs to go visit family or some mutual friends that she knows you trust."

Steele shook his head. "She never goes anywhere without me."

"Then let me ask you this. Does she leave the children with a sitter or a girlfriend on a regular basis for several hours at a time?"

"No, Randi is always with the children. She does leave them with a sitter every now and then, but not that often."

"Okay, then let's try this. Does she leave the room to make telephone calls or have conversations outside of your hearing?"

"No. But I thought you said your wire taps didn't show anything anyway."

"Our wiretaps didn't, but most adulterers have figured out how to use prepaid telephone cards and public telephones."

The two men sat in silence watching Travis play with the other children on the playground. "Father Austin, do you have a pattern of being away from home on a regular basis that she can depend on?"

"Like what?"

"Well, many men have certain things that they do on a regular basis. Some play golf on the same day at the same time. Others go fishing on the same day and time. One man we worked with spent every

Sunday night and Monday at his lake house. A woman involved with a paramour will take advantage of the times that they know their husband will be otherwise occupied."

Again, Steele shook his head. "No, I work. Randi can always find me, but she really never knows when I might show up at the house."

"One last set of questions. Has your wife changed her hair? Has she gone on a diet and lost weight? Have you found suggestive underwear or lubricants? Has she developed a new appreciation for some type of music that she never listened to before? Have you noticed that she has an abundant supply of breath mints or sprays? Or is she wearing a new perfume?"

"No, none of those things."

"Does she have a friend or group of friends that you don't know?"

"No, no. A thousand times no. None of those things apply to Randi. What difference do they make?"

"Because those are all the patterns of adulterers. Your wife simply does not fit the pattern. Further, the vast majority of adulterers become involved with someone that their spouse has met or at least knows exist. Father Austin, your wife simply does not fit the pattern and the past couple of weeks has further verified that."

Steele took in a deep breath. It was then that he realized that he hadn't even been breathing during the questioning. He glanced over at Travis and then he dropped his head and looked at the ground in front of him.

"You're not disappointed, are you?" Tim had a puzzled look on his face.

"Oh, no. Please understand. When I hired you I was hoping that you wouldn't find anything. The last thing in the world I wanted was to discover that my wife was being unfaithful to me."

"Well, Father Austin, I need you to understand that I'm not saying she hasn't been."

"But I thought..."

"You're forgetting the original reason you called me."

Steele threw his head back and shut his eyes. "Oh, those damn pictures."

"I'm afraid so. We still have these pictures. But we've discovered some things about them that you might find interesting."

"Oh?"

Tim opened the briefcase that was sitting on his lap. He took out the pictures. Now take a critical look at these pictures. Do you notice anything?"

Steele took one of the pictures from him and studied it yet one more time. He shook his head. "Tim, I've looked at these pictures over and over again. They are what they are."

"No, that's where you're wrong." He placed all three pictures on the bench in between them. Look at the man's face."

Steele studied the picture again. He started shaking his head.

"You don't see it?"

"I don't see anything but the pleased look he has on his face."

"Exactly!" Tim almost shouted. "I didn't see it either, but one of my photographers did. He pointed it out to me. The man is posing. Now, look at the direction he's looking."

"He's looking straight at us."

Tim started chuckling. "No, Father Austin. He's looking into the camera. The man knew where the camera was. He's posing. He's posing for the camera. Do you know what that means?"

Steele was perplexed. "Help me."

"Father Austin, look at your wife. She's oblivious to a camera being present. She has no idea she's being photographed. The man, on the other hand, knows and is looking directly into the camera."

"Tim, I hate to be so dense, but what are you telling me?"

"Father Austin, our hunch is that your wife was being set up. "

"So does that mean these are perfectly innocent pictures?"

Tim started putting the photographs back in his briefcase. "No, I didn't say that. I just said that she could have been set up. We just don't know how she might have known this guy."

"Do you know anything about him?"

"Information comes to me during an investigation in some of the most interesting ways. My photographer and I were studying these pictures when my receptionist walked into the office. She was bringing me my telephone messages. Anyway, she spotted one of the photos and exclaimed that she knew the guy."

Steele felt his heart skip a beat. "Who is he?"

"Now don't get too excited. It seems my receptionist likes to go up to Atlanta from time to time to one of those male strip clubs. This guy is a dancer in one of those clubs. He also does some modeling. And..." Tim chuckled. "Men or women can hire him as an escort."

"So he's gay."

"Can't quite figure that one out. He often goes home with women after his strip show. He may be a bisexual. We didn't investigate his escort calls, but we couldn't help but discover he is rather popular with the ladies."

Once again, Steele felt a dark cloud wash over him. "Tim, what does all this mean? Where do we go from here?" Amanda began to stir. Steele reached down and patted her on the back. She appeared to be going back to sleep. Travis was now on the merry-go-round with a couple of other children.

"Father Austin, have you thought about asking your wife about these pictures?"

Steele nodded.

"Then could I ask you why you haven't?"

"I guess I'm afraid of two things. First, I'm afraid she'll lie to me and then I'll find out that she did lie to me. Or, she'll tell me she did have a liaison with this guy. Either way, it could spell the end to my marriage." Tears filled Steele's eyes. "See these little children. I just don't know if I could take them through the pain of a divorce. I don't want them to have a weekend dad or mom. I don't want every other Christmas and birthday with them."

"So divorce is out of the question for you?"

"I don't know. How can a man ever take back a woman that's allowed another man to be inside her? How can he ever want to make love to a woman that's allowed another man to do all those intimate things with her? Do you really want a wife back that has gotten naked for another man? I preach forgiveness all the time. I just don't know if I can practice it."

"According to our wiretap your wife is already afraid that your marriage is in trouble."

"After seeing these pictures, my feelings toward her have changed. There's no question about that. She's not as attractive to me. I don't find her sexy any more. I have to force myself to even hug her or kiss her. I just don't trust her. It's hard for me to be vulnerable with her."

"But we don't have any proof that she's done anything."

"Exactly. Can you imagine how my love for her is going to change if you do? Just look at what these suspicions have done to me and my feelings for her."

"I'm sorry, Father Austin. My heart goes out to every man or woman that I've ever worked with in this situation. My heart goes out to you."

"So what now?"

"Well, in all honesty I think you need to save some of your money. I don't think following her or doing a wiretap is going to produce anything."

"Then what?"

"My receptionist sometimes does some field work for us. She's quite a looker. She'd like to take a crack at the guy in the photos. She thinks that if she plies him with a combination of liquor and hormones she just might be able to get the truth about these photos out of him."

"And you think that'll work."

"If it doesn't, I can always have a couple of my men lean on him."

Steele's eyes lit up. "Oh, I don't know if I can go along with that."

"How bad do you want an answer?"

"I have to know. These suspicions are killing me. They're destroying my family, and worse, they're destroying my love for my wife. I need to know one way or the other."

"Then Father Austin, you need to leave the investigative work to us. That's what you're paying me for."

Steele didn't like what he was hearing. He didn't like the plan. A new swell of anger rose up in him. He was furious at Randi for putting them in this situation.

Chapter 21

GARY HENDRICKS AND Tom Barnhardt sat huddled over their martinis in the bar of The Magnolia Club. They had agreed to meet there at four o'clock, knowing that the chance of anyone else seeing them from First Church was remote. The bar at the club didn't begin to fill up until after five o'clock. That's when most of the members would stop by for a beverage after they'd closed their offices and before going home. Their plan was correct. The bar was absolutely empty. The two of them and the bartender were the only ones in the room. Still, to be safe, they took a small table at the far end of the room and well out of earshot of anyone who might enter. "Congratulations, Mister Junior Warden." Tom Barnhardt smiled.

"So far everything is going according to plan." Gary Hendricks had been elected Junior Warden at the annual meeting.

"As Junior Warden, you're now in the position to speak for both the parents who are members of First Church and those that are not."

"Well, you and I both know that ninety percent of the students at the school don't belong to First Church and don't ever plan to belong to First Church."

Tom lifted his glass to toast Gary. Gary responded. "The church is holding the school back. We're never going to get the broader support of the community until we separate the two."

"You know it and I know it, but it's not going to be an easy thing to do."

"I've talked to a lot of people in this community. They're excited about the possibility of it becoming an independent day school. We've just got to figure out a way to get the rest of the Vestry to go along with us."

Gary nodded. "When I was Chairman I asked some of the real *movers and shakers* in this town if they'd serve on the Board. I was constantly turned down. As it's structured now, the Board is nothing more than a committee of the Vestry. No one worth their salt is going to want to serve on a Board that could have their decisions overturned by the Vestry."

"I tried to convince Austin of that. I even took a group with me to a meeting of the Vestry to convince them of it, but they did everything but hang me from the rafters. They wouldn't even consider the idea."

"Where do you really think Austin stands on the subject?"

Tom Barnhardt shrugged. "I've tried to talk to him about it on several occasions. I think if the truth were known he'd be all in favor of the separation. It would be one less thing for him to have to deal with. On the other hand, some of the old faithful in the parish are his strongest supporters and they're firmly opposed to the idea. I don't think he'll go against them."

"What about the Senior Warden?"

"Oh, he's going to be a problem. He and Ned Boone are bosom buddies. Ned is a formidable force and in complete opposition."

"And the Bishop?"

"As you know, he's retiring. We've got to get this done before the new Bishop even realizes what's happening."

True to his training as an attorney, Gary reached into his coat pocket and brought out a small tablet and a pen. "Okay, let's do a count. We know that the four new Vestry members will vote with us. We have my vote. That's five. We only need two more. "

"Forget Sparks and Stone. They'll never go along with it. There's no way we can get the Senior Warden's vote either."

"That just means we have to work on a couple of the other members of the Vestry."

A big smile crossed both men's faces. Then Tom Barnhardt couldn't hold back his excitement. "Let's have another round. I believe we're going to be able to do it. We need a fresh round to toast the new independent school in Falls City."

Gary nodded. "Yes, but I want it to remain an Episcopal School."

"That's fine. But let's make it an Episcopal School in name only. We don't want the Church exercising any control over it."

"Agreed, but I want there to be chapel services led by Episcopal clergy."

"I don't have any problem with all that. I just don't want the Church calling the shots. The board needs to be in charge. The board needs to be in control of the curriculum, finances, everything."

"That's the goal." The bartender brought them two more drinks. Gary took a sip of his drink. "But I'm afraid the Rector could be a problem for us."

"If he gets in our way, we join forces with Ned Boone and the Idles. It's common knowledge they're out to remove him. They'll welcome our help. They just won't know why we're helping them."

"And you think we can fool Elmer Idle?"

Ted Barnhardt let the laughter pour out of him. "Have you ever seen a more arrogant incompetent in your life? He's so full of himself that he wouldn't be able to see our plan if we put neon lights on it for him. He'll be so caught up in being a part of something that is bigger than he is that he'll lead the charge."

Gary smirked. "Yeah, but I'm going to have to convince him that I'm his friend and confidante."

"You can do it." Ted Barnhardt removed the spear with olives on it from his drink. He placed it on his napkin. He then turned his glass up and swallowed the rest of his drink. "The timing is perfect. All the storm clouds are gathering at the same time. There's going to be a new Bishop. Soon we will have a majority of the Vestry. Idle and Boone have been organizing the parish to dump the Rector. If we get rid of Austin we'll have a new green Rector. I'm telling you, the omens are all in our favor. I promise you that once we have a majority vote on the Vestry, First Church School will become separated from the Church and we'll be in control."

Gary Hendricks smiled. "At long last. My law firm will handle all the legal details." He was interrupted by the sound of a group of men coming into the bar. "I think maybe it's time for us to go. We don't want to be seen together just yet, but let's stay in touch."

Ted Barnhardt and Gary Hendricks left The Magnolia Club that day through separate doors.

Chapter 22

"STONE, I DIDN'T realize you represented plaintiffs in divorce matters." Henry and Virginia Mudd were gathered in the conference room in the law offices of Peter McKnight.

"I don't usually, but Henry here asked me to represent him." The two men shook hands. Stone looked over at Virginia. She immediately averted his gaze and busied herself rearranging her dress. "Hello, Virginia."

"Good Morning, Mister Clemons," Virginia uttered in a barely audible voice. Virginia did take a long hard look at Henry when he entered. He nearly took her breath away. She had forgotten how truly handsome he was. Now he looked so slim and fit in his dark blue suit. When he looked her direction she dropped her eyes to stare at the papers on the table.

"Virginia." Henry acknowledged.

She looked back at him, trying not to stare. "I hope that we can keep things pleasant this morning, Henry."

That struck Henry Mudd's funny bone. "Pleasant, hell, Virginia, you're counter suing me for divorce on the grounds of adultery. Have you and that slut Alicia been smoking wacky tobacco again? For God's sake, I don't know what you're thinking."

Just then Stone started tapping Henry on the foot with his own underneath the table. Henry looked over at Stone. Stone gently shook his head, indicating that Henry should be quiet.

"I suppose we should just get right to it." Peter McKnight reached for the stack of legal papers in front of him. He gave a copy to Stone and then a copy to Henry. The formal documents were conveniently stapled at the top to a blue background sheet. "These are the terms of Mrs. Mudd's countersuit. I'll give you just a few minutes to read them."

"Before we read anything, I want to know just where you get off accusing me of adultery, Virginia?"

Once again, Stone began tapping Henry's foot with his own. Henry threw his hands up in the air and slumped back into his chair. "I believe my client has asked a legitimate question." Stone asked calmly. "What evidence do you have that he has violated his marital vows?"

Peter looked at Virginia. She nodded. "I suppose we do need to discuss your client's infidelity first. Henry, do you know a Miss Delilah Cummings?"

Stone put his hand on Henry's arm. "My client does not have to answer your questions. This is not a trial and he is not your witness. This meeting was called at your client's request to see if we couldn't avoid a divorce trial and settle this matter amicably. We are here as a courtesy to your client and nothing more. I advised my client against this meeting, but he believed that it would be in the best interest of his children to try to avoid a court hearing. Now let's hear the substance of your accusation. "

Once again Peter looked at Virginia. Virginia nodded. "Mister Mudd, we know that you have been seeing Miss Cummings. We know that for a brief time she was a receptionist in your office. She is now a receptionist at the hospital. She is also a student in the night school of the local college. We know that you have been corresponding with her. We have copies of some of your correspondence."

Henry rose up in his chair and was about to speak when once again Stone put his hand on his arm and motioned for him to be quiet. "The last time I read divorce law, I don't believe that correspondence between a man and a woman that he is not married to constitutes infidelity."

"One of these notes suggests a relationship between your client and Miss Cummings that goes beyond friendship."

Henry had told Stone all about Delilah. Stone believed Henry had been honest with him and so he continued to refute the letters. "Do you have evidence of a physical relationship between my client and Miss Cummings?"

Peter McKnight countered. "Let me show you a copy of this note. In it your client expresses feelings that are totally inappropriate for a husband to write to a woman that is not currently his wife."

Stone was relentless. "Do you have any evidence of a physical relationship between my client and Miss Cummings?"

"The court will think that these letters certainly imply that such a relationship exists."

Stone leaned across the table toward Peter McKnight and looked him directly in the eye. "I'm going to ask you for the third and final time. Do you have evidence that a physical relationship exists between my client and Miss Cummings while he has been married to Virginia?"

"Stone, you don't want me to take these notes into court. You may not practice family law on a regular basis, but you certainly understand the significance of these letters."

Stone leaned back in his chair. He looked over at Henry. Henry could not help but see the glimmer in Stone's eyes. Stone knew that he had the upper hand. "Let's just have a look at your requested divorce settlement."

"Now you're being more reasonable." Peter McKnight smiled at Virginia. "Let me just give you the highlights. Virginia will retain the family home and furnishings. Henry will be able to remove his personal items. She will keep her Mercedes SUV. She will be given full custody of the children. Henry will have visitation every other weekend and alternate holidays. He may have the children for six weeks during the summer. Financially, my client will retain one half of all the current assets and will continue to receive one half of Henry's assets and income in his law practice for the rest of her life or until such time as she marries again. Of course, your client will be responsible for my fee, the expenses of my office, and any and all court costs. There are a few other minor settlement issues, but those are the highlights."

Stone looked at Henry and grinned. He stared at Virginia. She could feel herself shrinking into her chair beneath his gaze. An icy silence washed over the room. "This is a very interesting settlement offer." Stone could hardly contain his amusement. "With regards to the property settlement and the custody of the children, it's almost identical to ours."

"I'm pleased to hear that." Peter smiled. "I told Virginia that I felt Henry would be reasonable. You have a reputation in this town as being very much above board when it comes to your practice of the law. I admire you for that. And Stone, your reputation is impeccable. I feel certain that we're going to be able to come to a resolution that is satisfactory to both sides."

"Oh, I don't think we will." The grin on Stone's face grew even wider. "You'll need to substitute my client's name for your client's name in all the spots on the agreement regarding property and custody."

"Henry, you're not going to try to throw me out of the house and take my children away from me, are you?" The panic in Virginia's voice was difficult for her to hide. "I just don't understand why you can't see me for who I am. I'm a good person."

Henry smirked. "Believe me, Virginia. For the first time since we got married, I see you exactly for who you are. Anything that happens in this divorce is not my doing. You've done it all to yourself. You have no one to blame but yourself and Jacque Chappelle."

"Jacque Chappelle, the museum director. What's he got to do with this?" Peter gave Virginia a puzzled look.

Virginia's face blushed a dark shade of red. Stone glanced at Henry and then back at Peter. "I fear that your client has not been completely forthcoming with you."

"Oh?"

"She did tell you that she had an affair with Mister Chappelle, didn't she? I assume she also told you that she became pregnant in the course of that affair and subsequently had an abortion."

Peter looked over at Virginia who was now staring at the floor. She did not make eye contact with him. "You have evidence?"

Stone opened his briefcase that had been lying on the table in front of him. He pulled out a folder and handed it to Peter. Peter opened the folder and sorted through the pictures. "As you can see, these photographs show your client allowing Mister Chappell to have coitus with her. We also have their adulterous relationship on video-tape. In addition, we have recordings of their telephone conversations in which she tells Mister Chappelle just how much she detests her husband, my client, and her hunger to be with Mister Chappelle again. She gives some very colorful descriptions of just what she wants Mister Chappelle to do to her physically. She also reminds him to be sure and bring marijuana and other drugs to their trysts."

Peter looked at Virginia once again, but she did not look back. "Well, as you can see, I had no knowledge of this relationship." Peter tried to gather his thoughts. "So you have proof that my client made one mistake. As you and I both know, that's not all that uncommon in marriages these days."

"Don't go there!" Henry shouted.

"I beg your pardon."

"I said do not try to dismiss her adultery as some kind of mistake. And don't you dare try to suggest that it's a common occurrence. I loved this woman with all my heart and I was faithful to her for our entire marriage. " Stone tried to silence Henry, but this time he would not be silenced. "Virginia, you can believe whatever you want to believe but no part of my body ever entered another woman while we were married. I don't know how much clearer I can make that for you. But you broke my heart. You've caused me more pain than I ever thought imaginable. Now I just want this to be over with. I want you out of my life. I don't want to ever have to look at you again."

Tears streamed down Virginia's cheeks. "I made one mistake, Henry. It was a dumb mistake and I'll regret it the rest of my life. Why can't you forgive me? We can still have a future together. We can get through this. Our love is strong enough."

Henry sat back in his chair, staring at her in disbelief. He then looked at Stone. "Show him the rest of it."

Stone nodded and brought out three more folders from his brief-case. "These are all photos taken from adult websites. As you can see, they show your client engaged in sexual relations with three different men."

Virginia began to cry hysterically. Peter reached over and put his arm around her. "Will you gentlemen give me a few minutes with my client?"

Stone nodded. He and Henry left the conference room and walked out to the reception area. "How tough do you want to be on her?"

"Just present the agreement as you've written it."

"You don't even have to do that much."

"I know. I just hope she takes it. I really don't want my children to ever know just what a slut their mother is."

Stone shook his head. "Man, oh, man. She really had me fooled."

"She had everyone fooled. I was such an idiot for trusting her."

Stone punched Henry in the chest with his finger for emphasis. "Listen to me, Buddy. You were not the fool in this situation. Virginia's the fool. She had a husband who worshipped the ground she walked on. She threw it all away for a roll in the hay."

Henry grinned. "No, Stone. It wasn't just a roll. It was multiple rolls with multiple partners. I just don't understand why she didn't charge for it. That's the part that has me confused. At least the whores get paid."

Just then the door to the conference room opened. "Gentlemen, will you please come back in?"

When they entered, they noticed that Virginia had tried to reapply her makeup to cover up the redness of her eyes and cheeks, but it didn't work. She was obviously still distraught but for the moment had herself under control. Henry and Stone seated themselves once again at the conference table. Peter took his seat next to Virginia. "What are you offering?"

Stone once again reached into his briefcase and pulled out a stack of legal papers. "You'll notice that our agreement is not as long as the one you proposed. The property and custody arrangements are exactly as you proposed but only with my client retaining custody and the property. The financial agreement can be taken as a one-time cash settlement for a greater amount or a monthly allowance over the next three years for a lesser total. If your client chooses the monthly allowance it would end in the event she marries before the three years is up."

Peter pointed to the financial settlement numbers on Virginia's copy of the agreement. "Henry, I can't live on this amount of money."

Henry shot a disgusted look at her. "Virginia, people can and do. Most people live on a whole lot less."

"But Henry, I spend this amount on clothes each month. What kind of house can I buy for this?"

"You should have thought about all that before you decided to get naked for all those men. Do you really want all these photos and videos shown to a judge in a Falls City Family Court Room? Virginia, take it or leave it."

Peter McKnight stared at the agreement for a few minutes. "Stone, do you think we could amend the agreement to have your client pay my fees and costs to date?"

Henry stood. "Let's go, Stone. Peter, you are a fellow member of the bar. You are due some courtesy, but you should have done a more thorough job of vetting your client before you took her case. No amendments. Take the agreement as it is written or we'll see you in court."

After Henry and Stone had left the room, Virginia looked at Peter. "What should I do?"

"For your own sake and the sake of your daughters, I think you should sign the agreement. If you plan to go to court, you're going to need another lawyer. Virginia, you were not forthcoming with me. You made me look like a fool today in front of two of my fellow attorneys. Maybe you should try to find out just what it is in you that makes it impossible for you to tell the truth. I'd like to suggest that you get into therapy. You are one messed up woman. You need help."

Tears streamed down Virginia's cheeks. "Where do I sign?"

Chapter 23

THE REVEREND CANON Sean Evans had grown up in a devout Roman Catholic family. He was the youngest of eight children. He'd been well educated in St. Mary's Parochial School. His mother attended Mass each day. The family recited the Rosary together every Friday evening before dinner. The reasons for Sean leaving the church of his childhood are many and complex. A lot is due to the broader education he received at Florida State University in Tallahassee. There he was exposed to critical thought. The history of the world's civilization was presented with some distinct differences from that which he'd received in the parochial school. Then there was the social life that opened up new possibilities that he'd only known in his dreams.

To say that Sean had lived a protected life would be an overstatement. He was encouraged to date nice Catholic girls from respectable families. The dates were not chaperoned, but they were limited by very strict curfews. His dating venues had been pretty much limited to social events held by the parish or the school. He had never really been given the opportunity to be completely alone with a girl. He'd held hands. He'd kissed his dates goodnight. He was only exposed to anything that came close to petting one time. Quite frankly, he didn't understand why it was such a big deal. At the University, Sean's world had been opened up in so many different ways.

When he announced to his family that he was leaving the Roman Catholic Church and entering the Episcopal Seminary to study to become a priest, his mother cried for weeks. She prayed for him to change his mind. She gave him books to read on the heretical English

Church. She reminded him of its bloody history and the fate of some of the wives of Henry the Eighth. Finally, she insisted that he talk with their parish priest

It was actually his boyhood Monsignor that gave Sean the best answer to give his mother. "Mom, you don't understand. I want to be married. I want a wife and children. In the Episcopal Church I can have both. You'll see, mom. When you come to Mass you'll think you're in a Roman Catholic Church or even better. We still kneel in the Episcopal Church. And I plan to make every Mass a solemn high Mass. I'm going to use incense and holy water every Sunday. Mom, we will even recite the Rosary. The only difference is that I'll be allowed to marry. I can be a father in the Church, but I can also be a daddy. Please be happy for me."

His mother attended his ordinations and received communion from him. She was first in line to receive a blessing after he was ordained a priest. When he became a Canon to the Bishop of Mobile, she was so proud. She bragged to all her friends that her son was in line to become a Bishop. She died last year. He hated that. He really wanted her to be present when he was consecrated a Bishop. She would not be there, but one thing was certain. Sean Evans believed he was just about to become a Bishop.

He pulled onto Bay Street in the historic district of Savannah. The Confederate Inn was easy to find. It lived up to its name. The white columns in front of the house and dark green awnings over the windows set it apart from the rest of the buildings. A valet parked his car for him and a bellman carried his overnight bag to the front desk. "Yes, Canon Evans. We have your room ready. Would you like to go directly to your room, or would you prefer to have lunch first in our dining room?"

"I'm meeting someone here for lunch. I'll wait for them at the bar."

"That's fine. Here is your key. Our bellman will take your luggage up to your room."

Sean Evans stopped in the lobby men's room before going to the bar. The room was empty. He stopped in front of the full-length mirror to look at himself. He liked what he saw. He had a full head of blonde hair. His dark tan accentuated his blue eyes even more. Sean worked out on a regular basis. He had wide shoulders and a narrow waist. He flexed his arm. He had perfected a nice set of biceps. He was not about to fall into the trap of turning into one of those priests with a big belly hanging over their belts. No, Sean took care of himself.

Just as he was walking out of the men's room he ran into Jim Vernon. "There you are. The desk clerk said that she thought you were in here."

The two men embraced. "Do you need to use the facilities?"

"No. I was just looking for you. Let's go get something to eat. I'm famished."

When the two had placed their order, Jim smiled. "Well, how do you think you're going to like living in Savannah?"

"Let's not get ahead of ourselves," Sean chuckled. "You haven't gotten me elected just yet."

"Sean, I'm telling you, it's a done deal. We've got our plan and all the players in place. You can order your purple shirts today if you want."

"Gosh, I'm trying not to get too excited. You know that these things can be pretty unpredictable. I know a lot of guys that have gone into the process convinced they were going to win, only to be disappointed."

"Sean, buddy. This is a solid plan. There is no way you can lose."

"Oh, I'm sure there's a way."

"Forget it, Sean. I promise you that you will be the next Bishop of the Diocese of Savannah."

Just then the waiter brought their meals. As they ate, they shared the latest gossip they'd heard about different parishes, priests and bishops. When they'd finished with their meal they each ordered coffee. "Tell me, Jim. What do you do to stay in shape? I can't believe you. You look fantastic."

"Me? Just look at you. I'm at the gym at least five days a week. I watch what I eat and I don't drink a lot of empty calories. I never touch the hard stuff. I just have a glass of wine from time to time. "

Sean nodded. "Well, it's working for you. I follow pretty much the same routine."

"With one big difference. You're down in Mobile so you obviously get to the beach more often than I do. You have a great tan."

"I try to run on the beach three or four days a week. That helps me keep my tan."

"And look at those guns. Your arms really look good."

"It's actually my favorite exercise. I love to do curls. I guess that and chest presses. Both of them work for me."

"There is one thing that we've got to be clear on."

"Oh."

"Okay, Sean. This is a very conservative Diocese. Like me, you're single."

"I've wondered about that. How will they receive a single Bishop?"

"I don't think it'll be a problem at all. Rufus Petersen is single. You just have to address the homophobes in the Diocese and assure them that you're on their side. Just tell them what they want to hear."

"But I thought things were changing up here. I keep hearing about that Rector out in Falls City. What's his name?"

"Austin. Steele Austin."

"I thought he was striking a blow for the gays."

"Sean. He's a jerk. There's a group in that parish that have been trying to get rid of him from the day he arrived. One of the first things we've got to do is join forces with them. He has to go."

"How big of a group is it?"

"Oh, Austin tried to tell me that there are only a handful of malcontents stirring up trouble. He estimated there were only four or five of them. But you and I both know how that works. Trouble in a parish may start out as a small fire, but by the time we hear about it in the Bishop's office, it has become a full-blown wildfire that's out of control. Austin may try to play it down, but we know better. His time has come. We've got to work with those parish leaders to move him on."

"Well, it doesn't sound like that should be all that difficult."

"Oh, I don't know. Stuff just rolls off him like water off a duck's back. I've never seen anything like it in my life. I think the guy is surrounded by an invisible armor plate."

"Maybe he would be an asset. Maybe we could use him to open up some of the minds and hearts of the conservatives."

"Forget it, Sean. Parts of the South are changing. This Diocese is not one of them and it's not likely to be one in our lifetimes. No, we need to play to the base."

"How do we do that?"

"The best defense is a good offense. You do exactly what I do. You preach against homosexuality, abortion, women clergy, and liberalism. You know the menu. Just tell them what they want to hear. If you do, they'll not only love you, but they'll throw money at you."

"Speaking of women clergy. Didn't Austin bring the first woman priest into the Diocese?"

"He did, and the people at First Church are not happy about it. Once we get that purple shirt on you, we need to work with the leadership up there to clean house. All the priests they have at First Church need to be removed."

"But Horace Drummond is one of the candidates for Bishop."

"Sean, that's a critical element in my plan. I supported his nomination on the committee and I'm publicly supporting him for Bishop."

"You're not going to give me the details of your plan, are you?"

"What you don't know won't hurt you. The only thing you need to know is that you're the next Bishop of Savannah. Have you picked out your Episcopal vestments?"

A broad smile crossed Sean's face. His white teeth glistened in the sun beneath his tan. "I brought a catalog with me. It's in my luggage up in my room. Do you want to go up and look at it with me? Maybe you'll have some suggestions."

Sean signed the meal ticket to his room. The two men walked up the circular stairway in the lobby to his room. Once inside Sean shut the door behind him. "I've been waiting for this. I didn't think that I was going to be able to wait any longer." He threw his arms around Jim and kissed him passionately on the lips.

"My God, you feel so good. I love having your arms around me." Jim unbuttoned Sean's shirt. He ran his hand over his chest, brushing his nipple. "Once you move to Savannah we can have each other any time we want."

Sean pushed Jim back onto the bed. "I'm only thinking about right now." He reached down and started unbuckling Jim's belt.

Chapter 24

"CRYSTAL, WHERE HAS everyone been?" Steele arrived at his office only to discover that none of his staff were in their offices. He couldn't understand. He'd looked in the conference room and library, but there was not a staff member in sight. He was sitting at his desk when he heard Crystal open her office door.

"Father Austin, your Senior Warden asked to meet with all the staff at eight o'clock this morning." Crystal blushed.

"He what?" Steele could feel his anger rise.

"He called us each individually last night. He told us that we were to meet with him in the undercroft of the church this morning. He said the meeting was mandatory and that if we failed to show we would lose our jobs."

Steele was on the edge of exploding. "And just what was the meeting about?"

Crystal's lower lip began to quiver. "Father Austin, I don't want to get between you and Mister Idle. He told us that if we discussed the meeting with anyone, including you, we would be fired."

Steele struggled to keep his voice calm. "Crystal, the Senior Warden does not have the authority to fire anyone. The staff works for the Rector and they report directly to the Rector. In the event that there is no Rector in a parish, the Bishop of the Diocese becomes the Rector. This is ridiculous."

Crystal was now on the verge of tears. "Father Austin, you know that my loyalty is to you. I'd be happy to tell you everything that was said, but I really wish that you'd begin with Mister Idle."

"Where is he?"

"He'll be here in a minute. He knows he has a nine o'clock appointment with you."

When Elmer Idle walked into Steele's office, he was all smiles. "Good morning, Father. "

Steele did not respond. He walked immediately to his office door and slammed it shut. "Just where the hell do you get off holding a meeting with my staff?"

"Now calm down, Father Austin."

"I'll not calm down! You have absolutely no authority to call a meeting of my staff. Further, you are completely out of line to mandate such a meeting. You have no supervisory powers over this staff and you do not have the authority to hire or fire staff. Do I make myself clear?"

"Now Father Austin, it was just a harmless little meeting."

"Have I made myself clear on your relationship with the staff of this church? They are employed by the Rector. They are supervised by the Rector and serve at the Rector's pleasure. Do you understand?"

"Now Father Austin, I was thinking it would be a good idea if I attended all the staff meetings in my capacity as Senior Warden."

Steele was tempted to walk over to where Elmer was sitting and give him a good shaking, but he feared he might not be able to stop there. He continued to stand in the middle of his office. "What part of *you have no authority over or responsibility for this staff* do you not understand?"

"Well, I am the Senior Warden."

"Yes, you are. And as such you have basically two responsibilities and no more. First, you preside at Vestry Meetings when I am not present, and when requested by me, you preside at the Annual Meeting. Your second responsibility is to report heresy and misconduct of the clergy to the Bishop. Beyond that, you have no other responsibilities."

"Now, Father Austin. I've upset you. I didn't mean to. Please sit down. Let's see if we can start over. I've been thinking of several things that I could do to assist you."

Steele walked behind his desk and sat down in his office chair. Normally, he would have moved the conversation to the sitting area in his office. He believed it was best to keep a desk between Elmer Idle and himself. He thought at this point Elmer would be safer. "Let's get some boundary issues settled. I am Rector of this parish. A parish can only have one Rector at a time. Anything with two heads is a monster."

"I understand all that. You just need to let me assist you. There are some areas of ministry in which you have a considerable deficit. I believe I could help you with those."

"I'm sorry, Elmer. I didn't realize you'd been to seminary."

"Now there's no need for that tone. I'm merely suggesting that there are some things that you don't do so well, and I am in a better position to do them for you."

Steele's anger gave away to curiosity. "Oh, like what?"

"Well, first, I was a drill sergeant in my military school. I was also responsible for organizing the chapel services. It's my observation that the clergy in this parish don't know how to lead worship. I would like to meet with them and teach them how to lead worship."

Steele sat in stunned silence. At first he thought that Elmer might be joking. He studied his face and realized he was serious. "You're not joking, are you?"

"Father Austin, if you'll just let me meet with the clergy for two hours, I can teach them how to lead worship in such a way that this congregation will respond as you've never before seen."

Steele was at a loss for words. In his entire life he'd never encountered such arrogance. He was actually sitting in the presence of a man with no qualifications to do so, who actually believed he could train priests of the church how to better say the Mass. "I honestly don't know how to respond to you."

"Then you'll consider it?"

Steele's curiosity was getting the best of him. "Just where would you begin?"

"Well, the first thing I would do is to instruct them to announce all the page numbers. Every time we go to a different page in the prayer book, they should announce the page before proceeding."

"But the liturgy continues from page to page."

"That's right. Just stop and announce the page before going forward."

Steele sat staring at him in disbelief. "Is that all?"

"Oh, no. The organist should also be trained."

"Continue."

"Well, he should come to a complete stop at the end of each verse of a hymn. That would give the priest the opportunity to shout out to the people the number of the verse we are about to sing."

"But we sing all the verses of a hymn."

"Well, we don't have to. That's something else I was going to talk to you about. Why don't we just sing the first and last verses of the hymns?"

"Because hymns are complete thoughts."

"I don't follow."

"The hymns were written as complete thoughts. To sing only the first and last verse would be like reading only the first and last paragraphs of a short story or the first and last lines of a poem."

"Is there anything else?"

"Several things."

"I'll tell you what. You write them down for me and I'll give them some consideration, but I can tell you right now some of them won't be acceptable. Maybe none of them will be accepted."

"But I can explain them to all the priests when we meet to do my training."

Steele took in a deep breath. "Elmer, you will not be meeting with the priests and you will not be training them. That is not your responsibility."

Elmer sat back in his chair and stared at Steele. "You're making a mistake."

"Maybe I am, but it's mine to make."

"You make enough of them already. You don't need another." Elmer shot back.

"You really don't like me very much, do you, Elmer?"

Elmer shrugged.

"No, that's not going to do. We have to work together as Rector and Senior Warden over this next year, so let's clear the air."

Elmer glared at Steele.

"Just what is it about me you don't like? Have I ever said or done anything to you or to Judith that was disrespectful?"

"No, not directly to us or about us."

"Then what is it that you don't like about me?"

Elmer shuffled in his chair. "Okay, you asked so here it goes. I don't respect you. I don't respect your style of leadership. I don't approve of what you've done to my church. And quite frankly, I don't think you are very spiritual person."

"Well, that's quite a mouthful. Do I have any redemptive qualities?"

"Father Austin, let's just say that I don't care for you and leave it at that."

Steele smiled. "No, I want to know if there is anything about me that you can find acceptable. Perhaps my hair?"

Elmer shook his head. "No, you wear your hair too long."

"Oh, then how should I wear it?"

Elmer pointed to his own balding military cut. "Like mine."

"But I have no plans to enlist in the military."

"This is a man's haircut. You look like you have to get yours done at a beauty parlor."

"So as far as you're concerned, there's nothing about me that can be admired?"

"You said it."

"I suppose you have some thoughts on the way I manage my family as well."

"Father Austin, you asked the questions so I'm going to give you my answers."

"Go ahead. Let's know exactly where we stand."

"I think both you and your wife are materialists. Look at your lifestyle. It's not befitting a spiritual person. You've bought that big house. Your wife drives a flashy car. People see you out at fancy restaurants. It's just not right that the church's money be spent living so extravagantly.

"But I don't spend the churches' money. I buy those things with my money."

"Let's not quibble over words. We pay you with church funds and then you live like a television preacher."

"True, you pay me a salary, but as soon as the check is cut, it's my money to spend as I choose. It is no longer up for committee consideration."

"Well, that may be the way you see it, but the people of this parish see it differently."

Steele was ready to draw this meeting to a close. "Anything else?"

"Now that you asked, your wife's clothes. She dresses far too fashionably to be a priest's wife. I don't know how you afford her wardrobe. I can't afford to dress Judith the way you dress your wife."

"Elmer, I don't know what you can or cannot afford, but if you can't afford clothes for your wife, maybe you should take that up with your employer. If you're having financial difficulties, lowering my salary won't solve your problems. My salary has nothing to do with what you earn."

"Now just a minute. Judith and I tithe ten percent of our income. We don't give it all to this church because of you. And to put your mind at ease, I earn four times what you do, but I earn it the old fashioned way. I work for it."

"And you're saying that I don't?"

"I think you're grossly overpaid for what's basically a weekend job."

"You really have no idea what is required of a priest, do you?"

"I have eyes. Now back to your wife's dresses."

Steele interrupted him. "No, Elmer. My wife's clothing is of no concern to you or anyone else in this parish."

"Well, you just need to know that the women of this church talk. Your wife doesn't want them to get down on her, but I fear it may already be too late."

"And what makes you say that?"

"Well, quite frankly, your wife is a flirt. The women of this church don't like it and you'd better get her under control."

Those words went right to Steele's heart. He tried not to let it show. "So, in one word, can you name one good quality that I might possess?"

" You have none. Part of that is not your fault. After all, you've never had to live in the real world."

"The real world?"

"You clergy all live in a Sunday School world. You don't have to deal with the challenges that those of us who have to work to earn a living face every day."

"So you think priests live in some sort of a bubble?"

"You said it."

"Interesting. Now, let me tell you about what happens in my bubble. I have to take the five dollars that too many of our people put in the offering plate and try to buy fifty dollars worth of goods and services with it. I am the one that tries to help people make sense out of the bad diagnosis they just got from their doctor, or when they lose their jobs or their marriages fall apart. I have knocked on more doors than I care to count in the middle of the night to tell a family that a loved one has just died. If I never have to go into another neonatal unit and baptize a dying infant, that will be just fine with me as well. For that matter, I don't know how many more graves of anyone I can stand over before I ask to be pushed in. And then, I have to sit in my office and listen to people like you complain about how loud the organist plays, the number of verses we sing in hymns, and whether or not the free coffee at last Sunday's social hour was hot enough. Frankly, Elmer, if the bubble you assume I live in is not the real world, then I don't know what is."

"I think you're being a bit melodramatic. I think all you priests have it far too easy. You work on Sundays for sure, you attend a few meetings and make a couple of hospitals calls. In the real world I would call that a weekend job."

Steele sat in silence for a minute just staring at Elmer. "Well, it's going to be a rough year. Isn't it?"

"There is one thing I think we can agree on."

"Oh, pray tell. Is it bigger than a bread box?"

"I want to help you get Dr. Drummond elected as our next Bishop."

"What? I thought you didn't approve of him or his ministry."

"Oh, Father Austin. This won't be about him. It'll be about First Church. One of our priests will be made a Bishop. That will earn our parish the reputation of being a Bishop Maker. Do you have any idea just how excited the people of this congregation already are over that possibility? I plan to work day and night to make sure the next Bishop of this Diocese comes from First Church. That's going to be some feather in our cap."

"I've got to tell you that really surprises me."

"That's because you don't understand our ways. You're an outsider. First Church is about to make history. Dr. Drummond will put us on the map. We'll play a very important role in the historical archives of this Diocese. Heck, we'll even be mentioned in the history of The Episcopal Church. First Church is not only going to give the Diocese a Bishop, but we're going to give the Diocese the First African American Bishop. That's really exciting."

"You've really caught me off guard. I didn't expect you to react that way."

"Like I said, you don't understand our ways."

"So how do you plan to help?"

"Well, I am a delegate to the convention to elect the next Bishop. Judith and I want to have several large parties for Doctor Drummond. We're going to invite all the delegates and clergy from the other congregations to attend. We want them to meet him and have a chance to get to know him. Horace Drummond will be the next Bishop of this Diocese or my name is not Elmer Idle."

Steele stood and extended his hand to Elmer. "Let's just put everything else aside and join forces to do that very thing. I think Horace will make a wonderful Bishop, and it will be my pleasure to work with you to make that happen."

Elmer took Steele's hand and shook it. He gave Steele a Cheshire Cat smile.

Chapter 25

THE NEWS OF Henry Mudd's divorce from Virginia spread through the streets of Falls City like a brush fire consuming the dry pine needles on a hot South Georgia night. It appeared first under the legal notices in the local newspaper. The curious immediately called the courthouse to get a copy of the decree. They wanted to know all the details. They would want to be the first to know on what grounds Henry had filed for the divorce. Then they would want to know the terms. How much did Virginia get? What would the custody arrangement be for the children? Henry had wisely asked the court to seal the records of his divorce. The details were not open to the public purview. Of course, that didn't mean that the details would be free of speculation and gossip.

"He filed for divorce against her, you know. When a husband files for divorce against his wife, it can mean only one thing. She was cheating on him."

"No, I fear you have the wrong information. A very reliable source told me that she has a drinking problem. If you'll notice she's not been around the church for weeks. That's because she's out in California at the Betty Ford Clinic. He took her out there himself to get her dried out."

"Well, that would explain a great deal. You know that he's still living in the family home with the children. A father doesn't get custody of the children unless the mother has really done something bad."

"Well, I never thought she was a very good mother anyway."

"That's true. That's so true. Henry was always with those girls. They absolutely idolize their father."

Henry knew that there would be gossip. For the girl's sake, he never wanted them to know the details of just why he'd divorced their mother. He'd resolved that he would never say a bad thing about Virginia to his girls. He'd further resolved that he would go to great lengths to see that his children continued to have a relationship with their mother. His prayer was that she'd clean up her act so that the girls would not ever discover just what a slut she really was.

"Now, Henry, I know that you're anxious to move things forward with Delilah, but I need to give you some words of counsel." Stone Clemons was filled with wisdom and Henry knew it. He listened to him carefully. "You need to continue to keep your relationship with her on the sly. You mustn't bring her into the public eye too soon."

Henry knew that Stone was right. "How soon? What would you consider a suitable time frame?"

Stone twisted his mouth as he contemplated the question. "At least six months and maybe longer. I would think that a year or two would be more in order. You need to let the gossip die down. You also need your daughters to have time to adjust to life with a single father."

"I know you're right, but Dee and I love each other. We want to be together."

"I didn't say you couldn't see her. I just mean you need to keep a very low profile with her. You need to be first seen as a broken man recovering from the trauma of a divorce or you'll become the swinging divorce'. As you are well aware, that could be damaging to you socially and professionally in this town."

"What about sex?"

Stone chuckled. "What about it? Personally, I'm all in favor of it. In fact, I rather enjoy it."

"No, Stone. Dee and I have been waiting until after my divorce from Virginia."

"That's between the two of you and God."

"If it's all the same to you, Stone, I plan to leave God out of my sex life. I don't think He's done me any favors. He sure didn't do much to stop my wife from screwing around on me."

"Get past that, Henry."

"Get past what?"

"Get past your anger. Move on. You've divorced Virginia; now enjoy your freedom."

"Well, let's have you discover that your wife has been screwing every Tom, Dick and Harry in town and see how fast you get beyond it."

"Henry, for your own sake and for the future you want to have with Dee or any other woman, get over it."

Henry nodded. "I know you're right. I'm working on it. Do you think I should introduce the girls to Dee?"

Once again Stone twisted his mouth thoughtfully. "You've been counseling with the Rector. I think that is a timing issue I would work out with his guidance. But for the foreseeable future I would advise against it."

"I don't want to have a clandestine relationship with her. I want it to be out in the open."

Stone pointed his finger at Henry. "Okay, let me tell you how this is all going to happen. First, you need to grieve over your divorce. Second, you need to give the single women in this town a shot at you."

"What?"

"Henry, you have a certain standing in this community and at First Church. There are lots of single women that are going to want to have a crack at you. If you just up and marry right away, they're not going to forget it. And you'll pay a price for it. Now listen to me. I know what I'm talking about. You need to put yourself on the market before you settle down with anyone."

"But I don't want to date anyone but Dee."

"I understand that, but you have a lot at stake here. You need to play the game to its logical conclusion."

"Can Dee be one of the women I date?"

Stone nodded. "She just can't be the only one. You can take her out, but not to the clubs and don't bring her to church. At least not until the time is right."

"So you really think that the single women in this town are going to pursue me?"

"Like a kitten on catnip."

Henry laughed. "Well, I'm not so sure that I believe you."

"You are a good looking guy. You are a man of means. You are the most desirable catch Falls City has seen in some time. You are the prize bull in the local cattle auction. Oh yes, the ladies will find you. You won't have to go looking for them."

Henry blushed with embarrassment.

"Just consider all that I've said to you. Play it smart. If Dee loves you, she'll understand and give you the room you need. Otherwise, if you bring her out too soon she'll be marked as the other woman. She'll be the slut that broke up your marriage. You say you love her. You don't want that for her."

"No, I don't. You're right. I need to follow your advice as much for Dee as for myself and my girls."

"Now you're thinking rationally."

What Henry didn't realize was just how fast the ladies would begin pursuing him. The very next morning he was sitting in the dining room having breakfast with his girls. He had asked Shady to move in and become a nanny in residence. She was happy to do so. The doorbell rang. Henry answered it. Standing at the door was Lucille Langdon O'Neil. She was wearing a low cut blouse with the top button open just enough to give him a hint of her ample bosom. The town gossip was that she'd had them enhanced. She had on a very short skirt that showed off her well-trimmed legs that received a serious workout on the Stairmaster most every day. In her hand was a platter full of freshly baked cookies. "Henry, I woke up this morning thinking about you and your girls being all alone over here, so I baked these cookies for them. Do you mind if I come in?"

Henry really didn't know what to do, so he stood back to allow her to enter. It was then he noticed that she was wearing four-inch heels to accent her legs even further. He just didn't know how many women got up in the morning and put on four-inch heels to deliver cookies. Lucille had already been married three times. He figured she was hoping to make him husband number four. Lucille stopped in the dining room. "Oh, you precious girls. Just look at how beautiful you are."

Henry's daughters looked at Lucille and then gave their father a questioning look. They each sank down in their chairs.

"Girls, please say good morning to Mrs. O'Neil."

"Please, Henry. I go by Miss."

"Okay, please thank Miss O'Neil for baking these cookies for you."

The girls muttered a *thank you* just as Shady came into the dining room. "I'sa takes these for you." Shady took the platter from Lucille.

"Oh, that's fine. I'll come back in a couple of days to get my platter."

"Yes'm, but I needs to get the girls to school right now."

"And I was just leaving for my office." Henry started walking toward the door. Lucille followed him. "But thanks for baking the cookies for us."

"Don't mention it. It's nothing." Lucille then extended her hand to Henry. He took her hand to shake it. She then put her other hand over his and rubbed it gently. She looked deep into Henry's eyes and whispered. "If there's anything I can do for you, please call. Anything, Henry. Anything at all."

And so it began. But Henry wasn't prepared for the dinner invitation that he'd received for that very night. Martha and Howard Dexter had invited him to join them for dinner in their home. When he arrived, he was surprised to discover that Martha's niece, Caroline, was visiting from Charleston. Martha seated her niece next to Henry at dinner. Martha spent the entire evening extolling the many virtues and homemaking skills possessed by her niece. That monologue was exceeded only by the one in which she pointed out all the things that Henry and Caroline had in common. When dinner was over, Henry's introduction to the single life entered yet one more phase. "Henry, would you please be a dear and drive Caroline to her hotel?"

"Of course, but I thought she was staying with you."

"Oh, I hope you don't mind, Henry. While Uncle Howard and Aunt Martha have a perfectly lovely guest room, I prefer to stay at a hotel while visiting relatives."

Caroline had also studied in the Lucille Langdon O'Neil School of Seduction. As soon as they were in the car, she crossed her legs and pulled her skirt up above her knees. "It certainly is a warm night," she announced as she unbuttoned the top button of her blouse. When they arrived at her hotel in downtown Falls City, the valet opened her car door. She immediately reached over and placed her hand on Henry's leg. "Henry, would you allow the valet to park the car? I would prefer that you escort me to my room. I mean, it is a strange hotel and I am a single lady and all."

Henry nodded and handed his keys to the valet. Once they were at her hotel room door she opened the door and smiled broadly at Henry. "I do hope you will come up for a nightcap."

Henry shook his head. "I'm sorry, but I really need to get home to my daughters."

She pursed her lips in a pouting fashion. "Oh, pooh. I was so hoping that we'd be able to get to know each other better." She ran her hands under Henry's jacket and rubbed his chest. "I was hoping we'd get to know each other real well." Then she whispered in his ear. "Please tell me you're not celibate."

Henry chuckled. "I've been married for almost two decades. That's sort of like being celibate."

"Well, we could change all that."

Henry took her hands and removed them from his chest. He smiled at her. "You need to understand I'm just not ready for any of this. The ink hasn't even dried on my divorce papers. You're a very attractive young woman and I'm sure there's no shortage of young men vying for your attention. Maybe we could try this another time."

"Well, I'm going to hold you to that, Henry Mudd. I'll be looking forward to my next visit to Falls City." She reluctantly closed the door.

Henry turned toward the elevator, ever so grateful for the wise counsel that Stone Clemons had given him.

Chapter 26

STEELE KNEW HE'D just been going through the motions. He felt so empty inside. He no longer had any fire in his belly for his ministry. He now had a Senior Warden that would be actively working to undermine him in the parish. The Bishop had all but disappeared from the scene and left the Diocese to Canon Vernon. Friar Mean was a good name for him. He'd already heard stories of clergy in the Diocese that he'd targeted for removal. He knew that this particular Canon was no friend of his either. He wasn't so sure about his new Junior Warden. He just didn't know where he stood on things. He played his cards very close to his vest and hadn't given Steele any indication as to whether or not he was friend or foe. Then he'd noticed that Tom Barnhardt and his family had started worshipping at First Church. He had already had a couple of confrontations with Tom. He wasn't so sure the Barnhardts would be a positive influence in the parish. He knew that he was a real take-charge sort of guy. It was his way or no way. Stone knew Tom Barnhardt's father. "I tell you that man has all the bad attributes of his daddy and none of the good."

Then there was his marriage. Steele had a difficult time focusing. Every time he closed his eyes, those pictures would flash before him. He found himself constantly wondering what Randi was doing. He was curious as to where she was and whom she was seeing. He'd started going home in the middle of the day just to see if she was there and if she was alone. He'd even found himself sneaking into his own house in an effort to surprise her. This entire thing was driving him crazy. He'd stopped eating. His clothes were just hanging on him he'd lost so much weight. He'd posed for a picture with a bride and groom. They sent him a copy. Steele hardly recognized himself. He looked so unhappy in the picture. He almost looked like a person that was desperately ill.

Crystal knocked on his door. "Father Austin, Mister Heatherington wants to know if you can meet him at the hospital. His eighty-seven year old mother is dying. He needs to take his father to see her. They both know that this may be their last visit. He would really like for you to be there with them."

Steele nodded. "When?"

"I checked your calendar and you're free for the next two hours. I asked him if now would be convenient. He agreed. They'll meet you there."

Steele arrived at the door to the hospital room at exactly the same time that Joe Heatherington and his dad arrived. He walked into the room with them. The elder Mister Heatherington walked to his wife's bedside. He leaned down and kissed her on the lips. She opened her eyes. In a voice just barely above a whisper, "Joe, I'd know those lips anywhere."

The son pulled a chair beside the bed for his dad to sit in. "These lips have kissed no one but you over the past sixty-five years."

"He took her hand in his and held it."

"We've had a wonderful sixty-five years."

"Yes, darling, we have. I don't regret a single minute of it. "

"I just wish that we could have a hundred years together."

"We will. We'll have all of eternity."

They sat in silence just looking into each other's eyes. It was as though no words were needed. They were literally reading one another's thoughts. Occasionally, he'd rub her hand or stroke her cheek, but no words were needed. Tears poured down their son's cheeks as he watched his parents have one last soul dance. Steele moved next to him and put his hand on his shoulder. His mother began coughing. The son pushed the call button for the nurse. "Maybe I could have just a small sip of water." The nurse poured it for her. "You're growing tired. We don't want our visitors to wear you out."

The elder Mister Hetherington nodded. "Maybe we should go, Honey, and let you get some rest."

She nodded. "If you say so."

He stood and once again kissed her on the lips. "You know I've loved you from the first moment I saw you."

"I never doubted it for a second."

He kissed her again. "We'll come back in the morning."

"Yes, Joe. I'll see you in the morning."

Steele then stepped up to her bedside and took her hand in one of his and held Joe's hand with the other. Their son held his mother's hand and that of his father. "O Gracious God, you have blessed this man and this woman with a life of love and caring. We bless you for this because we know that you are the source of all life and all love. We thank you that Joe and Mary found each other and built a home and life together. We thank you for their son, Joseph, and the love and life they share with him. Now just as you loved and protected the Holy Family, we ask you now to continue to bless and guard this family both in this life and the life to come." Steele then made the sign of the cross on each of their foreheads and blessed them.

Joe and Mary kissed yet one more time. He gave her a gentle wave from the door. She smiled and waved back. "I'll see you in the morning."

He smiled and nodded. "You can count on it. I'll see you in the morning."

As Steele drove back to his office, he thought about Joe and Mary. He thought about the life they'd shared together. He wondered if there had ever been a time in their sixty-five years when they'd doubted their love. He wondered if there had ever been a time when the one or the other had cheated with another person. But something about them led him to believe that none of those bad things had happened. They were much more than husband and wife. They were soul mates. Steele had thought that Randi was his soul mate. Now he just didn't know.

"Father Austin, did you make it to the hospital in time?" Crystal met him in the hallway outside his office door.

"Yes, but in time for what?"

"We just got a call from Mister Heatherington. He said his mother died."

"We all were just there. I figured it would be several more days."

"He wants you to call him."

Steele went immediately to his office telephone and dialed the number. "Joseph, I'm so sorry. If I'd known she was so near death I'd stayed with her."

"No, Father Austin. My mother did it her way. She was just hanging on long enough to say goodbye to us all. I knew it. My Dad was not surprised to hear that she'd died. It was as though he fully expected it."

"They really did have a unique marriage didn't they?"

"Oh, my parents really loved each other. There was absolutely nothing that the one wouldn't do for the other."

"It's really what the scriptures mean when they speak of love that loses itself in the beloved. The husband and wife become so devoted to each other that they begin to look alike. They even begin to sound the same and walk the same."

"You just described my parents. Can we do the service on Thursday?"

"No problem. I'll clear my calendar. Do you want to agree on a time right now?"

"No, let me call you tomorrow morning. I want to discuss it with my dad. We have a few out of town relatives we need to contact. I'll call you back tomorrow."

Chapter 27

STEELE HAD JUST gotten out of the shower. He had wrapped a towel around his waist and was preparing to go to his bathroom sink to shave. Randi walked into the room with the telephone in her hand. "Steele, it's Joseph Heatherington. He says he needs to speak to you right away."

"Joseph, is everything okay?"

"I'm sorry to bother you so early in the morning, Father Austin. I need to tell you something."

"Okay. Go ahead."

"Father Austin, my dad died in his sleep last night."

"What?" Steele tried to calm the surprise in his voice. "I mean, I'm so sorry. That's a lot for you to handle in twenty-four hours."

"No, Father. I'm okay with it. Do you remember what my mother said to my dad when he left her hospital room?"

"Yes, I do. I was really touched by it. She told him she'd see him in the morning."

"Yes. And do you remember that he promised he'd see her in the morning as well?"

"I remember."

"Father Austin, that's exactly what she meant and my dad knew it. He never disappointed her one time in his life. He wasn't about to start now." His voice broke. "They're together now. He made good on his promise to see her in the morning."

Chapter 28

HELEN, GEORGIA IS located in the Blue Ridge Mountains of North Georgia. It is a beautiful Alpine Village located on the Chattahoochee River. There are cobblestone streets and old world towers. The village is resplendent with shops and restaurants. Visitors can spend the day strolling the streets or idling in one of the many beer gardens overlooking the Chattahoochee. The more active can enjoy everything from water tubing to horseback riding. Henry had taken the counsel that Stone Clemons had given him seriously. He wanted to protect Dee. He did not want anyone in Falls City speculating that she might be the reason for his divorce from Virginia. For that reason, he had asked Dee to drive to Helen in her own car. He would meet her at the lodge. He did not want to risk having any of the gossips see them leave town together.

He had rented a room for them right on the river. They could sit on the deck adjacent to their room and look out at the river. Or, if they chose, they could sleep with the windows open and hear the water rushing over the rocks beneath their window. Henry wanted to make sure their first time to make love would be special. He had been waiting a long time to make love to Dee. He knew he wanted to take his time. He loved her. He knew that. Now he wanted to show her just how much he loved her.

Henry pulled onto the gravel driveway in front of the lodge. He parked his car next to Dee's. She would be waiting for him in the room. As he took his luggage from the trunk of his car he realized that his hands were actually shaking. He also knew that he was already aroused.

He was so anxious to possess her. He hadn't felt like this since he was first in love with…He dismissed her name as soon as it entered his mind. Henry locked his car and walked through the breezeway toward their room. His heart stopped. There standing at the soda machine was Dee. She was wearing tight white pants. She had on a white top that was as equally form fitting and accented her full breasts. Henry could tell that she was not wearing a bra. He simply froze in his steps so that he could just look at her. She was barefooted. He thought she looked absolutely adorable. He wanted to pick her up and carry her to the room. She turned her head and saw him. She ran toward him. He put down his luggage so that he could catch her. She threw herself at him, wrapping her arms around his neck and her legs around his waist. She kissed him passionately. He opened his mouth to receive her tongue. When their lips parted he started laughing. "I'm sure glad that you managed to land around my waist. I'm not so sure but what you could've done some serious damage if you'd landed a few inches lower." He put her down and held both her hands in his so he could look at her. "Damn, Dee. You are so beautiful."

"You look pretty good yourself."

"Did you get your soda?"

"I don't need it now. I have you."

He took her hand. He picked up his luggage with the other and started walking with her toward the room. "What do you want to do first? Are you hungry? Do you want to go get something to eat?"

She looked up at him. "No you don't, Henry Mudd. You've kept me waiting far too long already."

"Well, we can do whatever you want to do. There are so many things to choose from."

She let go of his hand and wrapped her arm around his waist. "I don't care if we don't leave this room all weekend. I want to get naked with you and stay that way. I only brought one change of clothes and I'm hoping that I won't need it."

Henry put his arm around her and pulled her close to him as they walked toward their room. Once inside, Dee sat down on the side of the bed. "Are you nervous?"

"Are you?"

He stood by the window looking back at her. "God, I love you so much. I just don't want you to be disappointed in me."

"Henry, why would I be disappointed?"

"Oh, I don't know. It seems like I wasn't enough for my wife. She was out there looking for greener pastures almost from the day we got married. Hell, I don't know, Dee. I told you I had a lot of baggage. Maybe I'm inadequate physically. I mean, I never thought I was. But then Virginia did what she did. She never initiated sex with me. Not one time in our entire marriage was it ever her idea. I always had to be the first to make a move. Even then she'd find all kind of excuses to keep me waiting. I don't know, maybe she got some sort of sick delight out of making me wait. Maybe she was hoping that if she put me off long enough I'd just give up and forget about having sex with her. Who knows what was going through her mind? One thing was certain and that was that she was not excited about doing it with me. I never felt like she really desired me. But then I saw those videos of her and the lengths she was willing to go just to be with those other guys. She was so excited to be with them. It was like she was really into them in a way she never was with me. Well, when I contrast her desire for her lovers against her lack of initiative and desire for me, I can't help but feel insecure. Maybe I'm a lousy lover."

Dee stood and walked over to Henry. She put her fingertips over his lips. "And you over analyze things. You need to keep two things in mind. First, I'm not Virginia. Second, I love you. If she'd really loved you she would never have slept with even one man, let alone all the others. I promise you, Henry Mudd, I will never hurt you. I love you and I want to be with you and only you. There's absolutely nothing about you that is going to disappoint me."

Henry put his arms around her and pulled her close to him. He kissed her again. She started unbuttoning his shirt. She ran her hands through the hair on his chest. She kissed his neck and his chest. She then unbuckled his belt buckle. "Let's take all this off."

Henry nodded. He sat down on the side of the bed and removed his shoes and socks. He then stood and took off his shirt and pants. He looked up to see that Dee was lifting the white top over her head. Her breasts were gorgeous. Her waist was so flat and trim. She looked at him and smiled a seductive smile. She then pulled her slacks off. She wasn't wearing any panties. She stood before him completely naked. "God, Dee. You're absolutely beautiful. You could have any man you want. Why me?"

She gave him a seductive smile. "Because I love you. I don't want any other man. I only want you."

Henry stood and took the couple of steps needed to get to her so he could embrace her. He held her naked body next to his. He never wanted to let her go. He wanted to lose himself in her. He kissed her again. He kissed her neck and shoulders. He bent down so that he could run his tongue over her breasts. He felt his hardness against her. He thought he was going to explode.

She took his face in her hands so that she could look at him. "Let's get on the bed. But I want everything off of you. That includes those briefs. He complied with her wishes. He removed his underwear and stretched out on his side on the bed. She lay down beside him. He once again began kissing her. He wanted to kiss every inch of her body. He loved the way she smelled. He loved the way she tasted. He worked his way from the top of her head to her feet. He rolled her over on her stomach and continued to smother her in kisses. He treasured every inch of her. He wanted to leave no part of her untouched by his lips. He rolled her onto her back. He pressed his face against hers. His desire for her was raging. He put his lips on hers. She opened her mouth to receive his tongue. He was just about ready to position himself over her so that he could enter her when she pushed him away. "No you don't, big boy. Now it's my turn. Lie there on your back and don't move."

Henry did as he was instructed. Dee began kissing him. She licked and gently bit his chest and neck, his biceps and his thighs. Never in his life had he experienced a woman make love to him like this. With Virginia he was always the initiator. Making love with Virginia had been a chore. She seldom moved and never made any sounds. She would just lie there. Occasionally she would run her fingertips over his leg or arm, but she never moved her lips and tongue over his body as Dee was now doing.

Dee was moaning. When he touched her just right with his tongue, she actually would give out a low scream. She whispered over and over again just how much she loved Henry. She told him the things she liked about his body. Then Dee did something that Henry had only seen Virginia do with other men on the videos. With him she had only wanted to make love lying on her back. Now, Dee knelt above Henry and gently guided him into her. She placed her hands on his chest and shut her eyes. Then she began to gently move above him. Henry watched her. He stared into her beautiful face. He put his hands on her legs. He loved her as he'd never loved anyone. Then to Henry's surprise large tears began streaming down the sides of his face and onto his pillow. For the first time in over a year, Henry Mudd was crying tears of love and joy. For that sacred moment he was one with Dee. For him, it was a spiritual experience.

Just maybe God had not forgotten him.

Chapter **29**

ROB AND MELANIE were Steele and Randi's best friends in the entire world. Rob had been a priest in Falls City at one time. He had been falsely accused of murdering his wife. Steele had been his friend and his pastor through the entire ordeal. Rob was cleared when his wife's own lover confessed to the killing. Melanie and Rob had met at a church conference in California. They had an affair. After Rob was cleared, he gave up his priesthood and moved to California to be with Melanie. They were married now. Steele, Randi, and Travis all had been in their wedding.

Randi and Melanie talked on the telephone every two to three days. Rob and Steele preferred e-mail with an occasional telephone visit. "Melanie, I don't know what's wrong with him. I just know that I can't live like this much longer."

"Has he completely shut you out?"

"Yes. He doesn't tell me anything. When he comes home he just crawls up inside himself. He either sleeps or watches television. There's so much distance between us. Some nights he doesn't even come to our bed to sleep. He just sleeps on the couch or in the guest room. When he does come to our bed he doesn't hold me. He stays as far away from me as the bed will allow. That's just not like him."

"Do you think he's depressed?"

"Melanie, I think that's a real possibility. I know that they're giving him a hard time again at the church, but that's nothing new. We've almost grown to expect it."

"Same old stuff?"

"Same old stuff with the same old people. The Idles, Ned Boone… oh, you know the cast of characters as well as I do. We do have a new player, though."

"Oh?"

"Yeah, Bishop Petersen is retiring, so he hired this new Canon that's a real piece of work. The clergy have all nicknamed him *Friar Mean*."

"Has he caused Steele any problems?"

"He's just let him know that he's opposed to most everything Steele is trying to do. I guess you could call that a problem when someone in the home office is undermining your ministry."

"Has he started being attentive to the children?"

"He's doing better. He took both of them to the park and zoo the other day. I think he reconnected with them. Travis loves his daddy and Amanda lights up with the biggest smile you've ever seen when he walks into the room."

"I just don't know what I can do to help you, Randi. You and I both know that the quickest way to destroy a marriage is to have one or both partners start distancing themselves emotionally. And that sounds just like what he's doing."

"I just feel like he's shutting me out."

"He's not angry?"

"God, I wish he would just get angry. He just gives me these blank looks. Sometimes he looks at me as though he's really hurt or wounded. Was Rob able to get anything out of him?"

"Not a thing. Steele just told Rob that everything was really beginning to get him down. He felt like he was burning out."

"Did Rob ask him specifically about me?"

"He did. And I hate to tell you, but Rob felt like Steele was pretty vague. He couldn't get him to be specific about anything."

"Do you think that he just doesn't find me attractive any more?"

"Oh, Randi. Give me a break. You're absolutely gorgeous. I can't believe that you've had two babies. I'm so jealous of your cute little figure I don't know what to do with myself. Don't you remember that young hunk hitting on you at the swimming pool when I was there?"

Randi smiled. "He was sort of cute, wasn't he?"

"Cute. He had the body of an Adonis and the face of a mischievous angel. And he was after you."

"Well, as flattering as that was, I wish my husband was after me in the same way."

"Randi..." Melanie was quiet for a moment. "Have you given any thought to the possibility...no that's silly. Forget it."

"What? What's silly?"

"Oh, I don't know. Just call it woman's intuition. But do you think it's possible that someone told Steele about blonde boy and you at the pool?"

"Oh, I don't think so. No one else was around that we knew."

"How can you be sure? You're a well-known face in Falls City. It wouldn't necessarily have to be anyone from First Church. In that town there are a lot of people that know you that you'd never recognize."

"But I chased the guy away."

"I know, but all of that could have been misinterpreted by a casual observer and then misrepresented even further to your husband."

"Maybe, but...no. I don't think that's the problem."

"Randi, something has turned the man who absolutely adored you into this zombie you keep describing for me. I think you should tell Steele about that incident."

"Oh, that was weeks ago. No, Melanie, I appreciate the advice, but I believe that what Steele Austin doesn't know doesn't hurt him. And I'm positive he doesn't know anything about blonde boy."

"Well, if you're sure. Is there anything you've said or done that would cause him to start distancing himself emotionally from you?"

"Almeda had me over for tea. She gave me a lecture on not being so flirtatious. Honestly, I never thought of myself as flirtatious. I just enjoy getting to know people. I like learning all about them."

"Randi, I'm your best friend. So let's be clear. I don't think Almeda was talking to you about having polite conversation."

"No. I guess not."

"Was she specific?"

"She says some of the women in the church are upset with me because I kiss their husbands."

"And how do you feel about that?"

"I don't think of it as a kiss. I just sort of smack them on the cheek and occasionally on the lips."

"Randi, I've seen you do that. Rob specifically asked me never to do anything like that. Are you really that naive?"

"I don't know. I guess I just didn't see any harm in it."

"Does Almeda think that's the reason Steele is distancing himself from you?"

"She didn't rule it out, but she thinks the primary problem is the way the people at the church are treating him."

"I'm not a marriage counselor nor am I a psychologist. I'm just your friend. But what I do know is that when a man or a woman distances themselves emotionally from their spouse it's because the other has done something to hurt them. They distance themselves so that they can't be hurt again. If it goes on too long then love will turn to apathy. The marriage is then over."

Tears welled up in Randi's eyes. "Do you really think that is what he's doing?"

"From all you've told me, it sounds like he is putting distance between the two of you. It sounds like he's been hurt and he's protecting himself."

"I don't want to lose Steele. I love him. I love our family. I love our life together, as awful as it can be in this parish at times."

"Then, Randi, you've got to get him to open up to you. You've got to find out just why he's shutting you off emotionally. If he won't tell you, then see if you can't get him to agree to go talk to someone with you. Tell him that you need to talk to a counselor and you want him to go with you."

"I know you're right. I also know I can't keep this up much longer. Something has got to give or I'm going to break."

"Don't break, Randi. If you love your husband, then you've got to fight for him. You fight for your marriage. You fight for your children."

"Thanks, Melanie. That's exactly what I need to do. You're a dear friend, and I don't know what I'd do without you. I love you."

"And I love you too, girl. Now call me in a few days and give me an update."

Chapter 30

"LADIES AND GENTLEMEN, we want to thank your for taking time out of your busy schedules to attend this meeting tonight. We promise not to waste your time." Gary Hendricks continued. "This is the fifth and final one of these meetings that Tom Barnhardt and I have organized. Tom, I'm going to turn the first portion of the meeting over to you."

"Thank you, Gary. As you all know, Gary has just been elected Junior Warden at First Church. He has previously served as one of the best School Board Chairs the school has ever had. Our plans are to elect him as Senior Warden at First Church next year." A polite round of applause was offered by the gathering. "I'm not currently a member of First Church. However, our family is in the process of going through the membership classes. But all of you know that I am a strong supporter of the school."

Gary Hendricks interrupted. "If I could just say one thing. Not only has Tom been a strong voice and generous contributor to the school, but he has also been the voice of reason in the midst of all the dialogue on separating the school from the parish. I want to thank you, Tom, on behalf of the entire school community for your vision and your hard work." Once again there was a round of polite applause.

"Gary and I invited all of you to attend this meeting because you are either a current or past school parent. We also know that your primary interest is in having a first rate private school in this community. Our current school is a quality parochial school. I think on that we can all agree. But we have to come to terms with the fact that the church is holding the school back. Those in charge of the parish have a limited vision of its possibilities. They would be content to have the school remain a parochial extension of the parish. Our vision is that the school will receive broader community support if it is an independent school."

Just then a man in the back of the room raised his hand. "Tom, I may not know everyone that goes to First Church, but other than Gary, I don't think that there are any members of First Church present here tonight."

"I'd like to answer that." Gary Hendricks stood. "We have organized these meetings specifically for current and past parents who are not members of First Church. We believe that if the school is to be successfully separated from the parish, we are going to need your support and assistance."

The man raised his hand again. "How? Doesn't the decision to separate the school from the parish ultimately rest with the Rector and Vestry?"

"Yes, that's true. That's where you can be of assistance."

The man shook his head. "How? We don't have a vote. None of us will ever be elected to the Vestry. We know that the majority of the students don't attend First Church, but other than helping with the occasional fund raiser and paying our tuition, I don't see that we have any role in the decision making."

Tom Barnhardt smiled and nodded at Gary. "I'll take that one. You're correct about everything you've said so far. But again, that's the problem. You've underestimated your power. The people in the community that write the tuition checks should have the final say in what happens in the school."

The man wrinkled his brow as several people in the group gave him a confused look. "Power? What power?"

Tom rocked back on his heels assuming the posture of a university professor. "Let's make a distinction between power and control. You're right. The Rector and Vestry are in control, but without parents to enroll children in their school, they have no power. Without us and all the people that attended the other four meetings, they have no school."

That comment brought several murmurs from the people in the room. There were many nods of agreement. "This is where we are on the articles of separation. As most of you know, Gary here is an attorney. He's drawn up some proposed articles of separation. Basically, what they will do is transfer all the authority for the operations of the school from the Rector and Vestry to the School Board. The Board will be responsible for and have control over all the fiduciary operations, the employment, and if needed, dismissal of the headmaster, the academics and all extracurricular activities. In short, the buck will stop with the School Board, which will be made up of community members, both Episcopal and non-Episcopal. The Board will decide and not the Vestry."

"But the current Board is made of both Episcopalians and non-Episcopalians."

"That's true, but the Rector and Vestry still have the power to overrule the Board."

Another man asked, "What about the property?"

Tom deferred to Gary. "There's not much we can do about that. All property in the Episcopal Church is held in trust for the national Episcopal Church. The Constitution and Canons are very clear on that and as an attorney, it's my legal opinion that the courts would uphold their right to title."

"Can't we get the parish to just deed the property and buildings over to us?"

Gary shook his head. "No, it's not as simple as all that. They can't do it without the Diocesan and National Church hierarchy getting involved. I just don't think that's going to happen."

An elderly man sitting in the middle of the room stood. His voice boomed. "I've been sitting here listening to all of this and I think it's important that the people in this room be reminded of some history. Some of you were too young to remember, but First Church stole its school from this community. The original vision for the school took place back when the integration order came down from the courts. Now, I don't want to debate the merits of all that. I just want to set the record straight. There were four of us. I was one of them that took the idea of starting a private school to Doctor Stuart when he was Rector of First Church. We took it to him because First Church was centrally located and it had the only Sunday School building big enough to accommodate a school. Some of you will remember this."

A woman raised her hand. "I remember it. My husband was one of the four men that were a part of that original group with you."

"I remember." He nodded.

"As you all know, we're Presbyterians but we wanted our children to get a good education. Our only hope after that integration order was given was to help the town start a private school. Well, my Paul is gone now, but he never got over the shenanigans that group over at First Church pulled. You're right. They stole that school from this community, and it's high time that we get it back."

"How'd they steal it?" A young woman asked. "I attended First Church School and I loved it. My children to go to the school." She shook her head. "I withdraw my question. I don't want to know. I just don't think it's all that important."

The man with the booming voice looked at the young woman. "Well, it's important to me."

"And to me." The widow of the other organizer protested.

"We were all supposed to go out and raise some seed money to help get the school started. We had a budget and knew exactly what was needed. We had a meeting to report our results. We all wrote on the chalkboard what we'd raised, but it just wasn't enough. So we decided to go back to the community and see if we couldn't raise some more money. We never had a chance to report the results of our work. At the very next meeting of the Vestry of First Church, the other two organizers that were members of that parish reported they'd raised enough to start the school without us. The Vestry chartered First Church School that very night. Our participation was no longer needed."

Those comments brought even more conversation to the room. "Before I sit down, I just want you to know that, in spite of that history, I enrolled my children in the school, and I've continued to support it all these years. I want to thank Tom and Gary for what they are doing here tonight. It's time that the church gave the school back to this community."

A man on the front row shouted, "What about the Rector? I hear he can be pretty stubborn. I'm not so sure that he'll go along with all this. It's my understanding we can't do it without his consent."

"Gary, will you answer that one?" Tom nodded.

"Well, if you haven't heard, there is a lot of unhappiness with the leadership style of the current Rector. I have reason to believe that he's growing equally unhappy with our congregation. Some of us believe his time has come. My hunch is that he'll be well out of the picture by the time these articles of separation are adopted."

"And the Bishop?" Another man asked.

Gary continued. "The Bishop is retiring. We'll have a new one. That's one of the reasons that Tom and I think we should get this process started right now. A new Rector and a new Bishop simply won't have enough investment in having the parish retain the school to give us much of a fight. When they see all of us coming at them, we think that they'll fold like a house of cards."

"Okay, then what makes you think the Vestry will authorize it?"

Gary smiled. "I'll toss that one back to you, Tom."

"Gary can't share this with you since he is Junior Warden and a member of the Vestry. Right now we only need two more members of the Vestry to support these articles."

"How can we help?"

"We've posted the names of the current Vestry on this easel. We've written the names of those that agree with us in green. We've written the names of the three that we know will not be persuaded otherwise in red. The names in blue are those that we think can be persuaded to vote with us, but that's where you come in."

Confused looks once again crossed the faces of those in the room. Tom continued. "How many of you know one of the people that have their names written in blue?" About half the people in the room raised their hands.

"Now how many of you know someone that has their name written in green?" Every hand in the room was raised. Gary and Tom smiled. "This is what we need you to do. We need you to use your social connections, your business connections, favors that you're owed. Cash in any chips you have with these members of the Vestry to persuade them to vote in favor of the articles. Put the pressure on them. If they're currently with us, help them strengthen their position. If they're open to supporting separation, pressure them into finally doing so."

"Do you plan to present the articles to this year's Vestry?"

"We haven't decided. It depends on how successful we are at getting the needed votes. Gary here thinks we should wait until after Austin leaves and there's a new Bishop and then strike. I can tell you this. When we take it to the Vestry, we will win. First Church School will become an independent school and will be governed by the people in this community and not the Vestry of First Church."

Applause erupted in the room.

"Now, lest you think we aren't giving you all the facts. We're not asking for the name to be changed. It will still be an Episcopal School, but it will not be a parochial school."

Again the room exploded with applause.

The man with the booming voice stood. This time his voice shook with emotion as he spoke. "Gentlemen, I want to thank you once again. At last, I feel like we'll get even with the founders of that school that betrayed us."

Gary walked to the man and put his hand on his shoulder. "As an attorney, I can understand what you're saying. But I want you to know this is not about revenge. This is about giving our city a first rate independent school."

The man nodded. "Nevertheless, the day that school becomes independent of First Church is the day that many of us in this town will finally feel vindicated."

His comment was met with a rousing round of applause and several pats on the back.

Chapter 31

"I'M TELLING ALL of you the man is convinced that I am his strongest sup- porter." Elmer Idle smiled at his wife, Judith, and Ned Boone. He gave a reassuring look to Canon Jim Vernon. They were all gathered at the Diocesan House in Savannah. Jim Vernon had requested the meeting. "I disarmed him by agreeing to disagree with him on Austin. I also gave him a half-hearted promise that I would give Austin another chance."

"Now, you didn't lie to Dr. Drummond, did you, Elmer?" Judith's eyes opened widely. "You know that Jesus does not approve of lying."

Elmer patted his wife on the hand. "Now, Honey. You know me better than that. I didn't lie to him. I was sincere when I said that my promise was half-hearted. I couldn't promise with all my heart that I would support the current Rector."

"Well, I would hope not. We've all agreed that he's the worst thing to ever happen to First Church."

"I have to tell you, Canon Vernon, that Elmer and Judith here have thrown some of the nicest parties this Diocese has ever seen. Ev- ery one of them was designed to drum up support for Horace Drum- mond to be the next Bishop of the Diocese of Savannah."

"That's just great." Jim Vernon smiled. "What about Austin? Is he on board? Do you think he believes your support for Drummond is real?"

Elmer shrugged. "He's a hard one to read. We've had a couple of difficult conversations, but I think I've convinced him that my sup- port of Drummond is self-serving. I told him I wanted to further the interests of First Church. I told him that while I wasn't a fan of Horace, we couldn't pass up the opportunity to make history for First Church. I think that's just the kind of twisted thinking he'd expect out of me." That statement gave the group a nice chuckle.

"And all of you are delegates to the Convention, right?"

"We are. The Junior Warden is the fourth. Horace Drummond will be getting all the votes from the lay delegates at First Church. We'll make sure Austin knows that. Of course, all the clergy will be voting for him as well."

Jim Vernon smiled. "I have to admit that Drummond made me a little nervous during the *dog and pony tour* of the Diocese. The man really is articulate. He has a great sense of humor. I was surprised at just how well he was received by the delegates."

"Well, not all the delegates were excited about him." Ned Boone frowned. "I talked to several clergy and lay delegates that simply were not impressed."

"Oh, even without our plan, I don't think he could be elected, but I don't want to take any chances."

"I think it was really unfortunate what happened to that one candidate. I felt sorry for him." Judith's voice actually sounded empathetic.

Jim nodded. "That was embarrassing for all of us, but we had to ask him to respond. The President of the Standing Committee received a letter from one of his former parishioners accusing him of misconduct. We had to ask him to respond. I for one believed him, but it was obvious that most of the delegates figured that if there was smoke there must have been fire. He withdrew his name."

"So we're down to four?" Ned inquired.

"We have the professional candidate, Horace Drummond, the other Deployment Officer, and Sean Evans."

Ned nodded. "I need to know a little more about Canon Evans. I want to make sure that we're not buying a pig in a poke."

"Mister Boone, as I told you before, you're going to like this guy. He's a traditionalist. He agrees with us on all the issues. One of the first things he's going to do is revoke the license of your female assistant. There will be no women priestesses in this Diocese. As for Austin and Drummond, they're history as well."

"What's his stand on queers?"

Jim Vernon tried to hide his own disgust at Ned's question. "He is solidly opposed. I've heard him say on numerous occasions that Jesus could heal those sick souls if they would only ask him. But the important thing is that when it comes to all the issues, he's in complete agreement with us. He's opposed to ordaining gays and he's opposed to gay marriage. I'm telling you that he's one of us. You're really going to like this guy. He's going to be a great Bishop. I look forward to working with him."

"He's not married." Ned pursued his doubts.

"No, Mister Boone, he's not. Like me, we are associates of a religious order. We've taken vows of celibacy. Quite frankly, I don't understand how clergy can divide their time between church and family. On this one, I believe the Roman Catholics have the right idea. Both Sean and I have given our lives to Christ and to serving His Church. Of course, there are times I wonder what it would be like to have a wife and children, but the Church is my life. I really don't want to be torn between the two. I've heard Sean say the very same thing."

Ned Boone was pleased. "Canon Vernon, I believe that not only are you the right man for this Diocese, but I'm excited to hear everything you're telling me about our next Bishop."

Canon Jim Vernon stood. "Okay, then. Everything is in readiness. Now at the convention, it'll be best if we aren't seen associating with each other. Understood?"

They all nodded their agreement. Canon Vernon opened his office door for them to leave. Judith stopped. "Aren't we going to end this meeting with a prayer?"

A surprised look washed over Jim's face. "Well, of course we should pray. Judith, will you lead us?"

Judith gave them all a pleased look. She extended her hands. "Let's hold hands while we pray." Judith shut her eyes. "Lord Jesus, we just lift up Jim and Sean to you. We know that you've chosen them to be the leaders of your church in this Diocese. We pray that you'll give us the strength to support them as they restore the true Gospel to our Church. We thank you that they will purify our ministry and once again bring priests into this Diocese that know you as their Lord and

Savior. We thank you that all the priests in this Diocese will once again be men of vision. Men that are committed to protecting our Church against secularism and the sinful ways of the world. We thank you, Jesus. We thank you, Jesus. We are so blessed. Amen."

Chapter 32

"FATHER AUSTIN, YOUR ten o'clock appointment is here." Steele pushed the intercom button.

"Send them on in." He stood to greet the two ladies that entered his open door.

"I'm Jaunita and this is Vera."

"Good morning, Ladies. Welcome. May I get you a cup of coffee?"

"No, thank you."

"Please, let's have a seat over here where we can be more comfortable." Steele indicated for the two women to be seated on his office sofa. He assumed his customary seat in his wingback chair. "Please excuse me if I have failed to put your names and faces together, but I don't believe you're members of First Church, or are you?"

The two women gave each other embarrassed looks. "Well, actually we don't attend any church." Jaunita looked at the floor.

"Well then, I guess you hide your cars in the garage on Sunday mornings." Steele chuckled. The two women gave each other questioning looks.

"No, I leave my car in my driveway." Vera answered.

Steele apologized. "I'm sorry. I was just trying to make a joke. I mean, here in Falls City if you don't go to Church on Sunday mornings, you could get targeted by the folks wanting to save you if they find out you don't belong to a church."

Once again the ladies gave each other a confused look. "No, that's not been a problem." Jaunita responded. "If I don't know who's knocking at my door I just don't answer it."

"Well, you are a wise woman." Steele smiled. "Now, tell me. What brings you to First Church? Are you interested in becoming Episcopalians?"

Once again the women appeared to be embarrassed. "Oh, no." Jaunita sat forward on the sofa. "'We're not here to join your Church. I'm a Methodist." She looked at Vera. "I'm not sure what Vera is. I think you're a Baptist aren't you?"

Vera was embarrassed. "No, I'm a Roman Catholic but I don't attend very often."

Once again Steele tried to make a joke. "Well, Vera. I wouldn't have been surprised if you had been a Baptist. You realize that the Baptists report that their membership in Falls City is larger than the population reported by the last census?"

Vera gave Steele a blank look. "No. I didn't know that."

"Okay." Steele made the time out motion with his hand. "I was just trying to be funny. Please excuse my poor attempts at humor. Now tell me. What brings you to First Church?"

Jaunita seemed almost apologetic. "Now, we don't want you to get the wrong idea. We're great admirers of yours. It seems like your church does more for the poor people in this town than all the others put together. Vera and I have talked about visiting your church. We're just not sure what to do. I mean, you all do all that standing and kneeling and bowing. We might get confused."

Steele laughed. "It's not as confusing as all that. Just sit behind a couple of folks and do what they do. You'll be okay."

Vera leaned forward. "Father Austin, we are both widows. Our husbands were in the military. We're members of the Legion."

Steele wrinkled his brow. "The Legion?"

"Yes, you know. The American Legion here in Falls City."

"Oh, the American Legion."

"Yes, we are in charge of our annual fund raiser. Each year we have this big event to raise funds for our soldiers. We put together gift packages of some necessities and a few nice surprises to send our troops."

"That sounds like a wonderful project."

Jaunita smiled. "I'm glad that you approve. The problem is that our event this year has outgrown our facility. We've already sold more tickets than our Legion Hall will hold."

"That sounds like a wonderful problem."

Vera nodded. "It is. But we're hoping that you can help us."

"How can I help you?"

"We were wondering if you'd let us use your parish hall. It would be more than adequate to hold our anticipated crowd."

"Well, it sounds like a very worthwhile project. I would think that we can accommodate you, providing we don't have anything else on the calendar."

The two women smiled at each other. "We already took the liberty of checking with your secretary and she said your hall was free the night we need it."

"Then it's just a matter of putting it on the calendar."

The two women once again gave each other embarrassed looks. "Well, there could be a problem."

"Oh?"

"Father Austin, we have a casino night planned."

Steele chuckled. "A what?"

Jaunita answered anxiously. "You know. A casino night. There will be poker tables, roulette wheels, dice. That sort of thing."

"Is that legal?" Steele asked.

Vera quickly responded. "Oh, we've already checked. We're doing it all for charity. All the money will go to charity. People will be given chips to play. They will turn them in for donated prizes. No one will win any money."

"Well, that all sounds innocent enough."

"Oh, it is." Jaunita nodded. "The people who attend will buy tickets. In return for their ticket everyone gets the same number of chips to play."

Steele spent a couple of minutes thinking about their request. "Is there anything else I need to know?"

Once again the women looked at each other. Then Vera dropped the other shoe. "Well, we want to have wine and beer available. It won't be for sale. Not for money anyway. People can purchase it with one of the chips they receive."

"And you've checked on the legality of that as well?"

The two women nodded.

"That shouldn't be a problem for the church. We serve wine at some of our social events. We even serve Irish Coffee after our services on Christmas Eve."

Vera and Jaunita gave each other big smiles. "Now, of course, we'll want to split our earnings with the church. Is a fifty-fifty split fair?"

Steele shook his head. "No, you're raising money for our men and women in the service of our nation. The parish will donate the hall to your cause."

"That just doesn't seem right. We want to give the parish something." Vera insisted.

"We'll do our own set up and clean up. You won't have to worry about that," Jaunita offered.

"No, I appreciate your offer, but I'll need to have my own custodial crew on duty to oversee everything."

"Then we insist that you at least let us cover their costs." Vera continued.

"Okay, I relent." Steele smiled.

"Jaunita, you said that you're a Methodist."

She nodded. "Honestly, I don't attend very often."

"Well, the Methodists believe in tithing. So let's just have you tithe ten percent of your earnings to cover the cost of the hall and my maintenance staff."

"Agreed." The two women responded simultaneously.

"Then all is in order. I'll have my business manager get in touch with you to work out the details."

As Jaunita and Vera were leaving Steele's office, Horace Drummond walked in. "Nice looking ladies." He hummed.

"And I'll do you the favor of not telling Almeda that you were leering at a couple of my visitors today."

"Well, you have to admit they were a couple of foxes."

"So it's true what they say?"

"What's true?"

"Snow on the mountain doesn't mean that there's no fire in the furnace."

"Just ask Almeda. She'll tell you herself."

"That is not the kind of talk I need to hear from my next Bishop. For God's sake, Horace, you're about to become my Father in God. You're going to be a successor to the apostles. "

Horace threw his head back and released his deep baritone laugh. "Whether or not I'm going to be your next Bishop is still to be seen. But I plan to continue to be just who I am, and you know who I am almost better than any other person I know."

"Okay, you win. What's on your mind?"

"We've got to do something about Easter Services." Horace handed Steele a sheet of paper. "Here are the attendance figures from the last three years. Look at last year. We had three services in the big church and two in the chapel. We still had people leave because there was no room for them in the garden. "

"I'm way ahead of you. I've got an idea. I'd like to add a Saturday night service."

Horace shook his head. "That may peel a few folks off, but I think most people will still want to come on Sunday morning."

"Not if we do it right."

"Go on."

"I want to advertise the Saturday night Mass as a Gospel Mass."

"A what?"

"Now hear me out. I've been talking to Josiah Williams."

"The black preacher?"

"Just a minute, my brother." Steele smiled. "Josiah Williams is my friend and I believe the politically correct term is *African American preacher.*"

Horace chuckled. "Lord, deliver me from politically correct white preachers."

"And you dare to include me in that group."

"Okay, get on with it. You have my attention. What have you and Josiah been talking about?"

"I've asked him to loan me his choir for our Saturday Night Easter Mass. Horace, they're fantastic."

Horace let out a long whistle. "Steele, were you born with some sort of death wish? This place will never tolerate having a choir full of black folks lead their Easter Service. Brother, you really need to think this one through."

Steele smiled. "Horace, I have and I really think it'll work. Josiah's choir is incredible. They do things with two pianos, an organ, drums, guitars, trumpets, and synthesizers. Hell, Horace, I think they're good enough to be on television. I think if we advertise it correctly and really promote it, we'll not only bleed off some of the Sunday morning crowd to make room for others, but we'll bring in an even larger group of visitors on Saturday night."

Horace gave Steele a long, silent look. "Tell me this. Just how much pot did you smoke in college? Because I think it either totally messed up your mind or it turned you into a creative masterpiece."

"So you agree?"

"I hate to say it, but I think I do. I think it just might work."

"Good, because I want you to be the celebrant."

Horace let out a big groan. "Steele, now I know you're nuts. You're going to ask the white folks in Falls City, Georgia to celebrate Easter on a Saturday night in a service led by a black choir with a black priest leading the service. Let's go back to that death wish question."

"Oh, I plan to be there. And I'm going to ask Ginnifer to be there as well."

"Now let me paint the full portrait for you. My dear Father, I don't think you're getting it. Falls City, Georgia. Exclusive First Church with Episcopal in parenthesis. White People. Black Choir. Black Priest. White Woman Priest and One Very Naive White Boy –slash – Crazy Half-Breed Indian from Oklahoma. Do you see any problem with this picture?"

"Horace, you've left out a very critical component"

"Oh?"

"The power of the Holy Spirit. If we keep doing the same thing in the same way year after year nothing is going to change. I promise you this is going to work."

"Well, you're the boss, but I'm beginning to understand why Rufus Peterson wasn't all that fond of having you in his Diocese." Horace released his deep baritone laugh one more time. "Hell, I'm not so sure I want you in mine."

"And now you're sounding more like a Bishop than a parish priest trying to make a difference."

"Well, let's just say that I am beginning to look at things from a different perspective."

"Horace this will be your last Mass as a parish priest. The next week you'll become our Bishop-elect."

"I'm not as sure as you are about that."

"Look, Horace. You have the support of the majority of the clergy in this Diocese. What I find even more amazing is that you have the support of the Idles, the Boones, and a lot of the bigots in this congregation. I never dreamed that would even be possible."

"Well, we'll see. You know as well as I do anything can happen in one of these elections."

Horace sat quietly looking out of Steele's window. His gaze fell on the First Church tower and the big magnolia tree that sat on the front lawn.

Steele watched his beloved friend lost in his own thoughts. "What's on your mind?"

Horace looked back at Steele. He was obviously reaching out to him. "Steele, I'm going to ask you a question and I don't want you to give me some BS answer. You owe me an honest answer."

Steele nodded. "Okay."

"Are you and Randi having marriage problems?"

The question pierced Steele's heart. He started nodding even before he was aware that he was doing so.

"What's going on?"

"We're just going through a rough spot right now."

Horace glared at Steele. "No, your marriage is in trouble. Randi has talked to Almeda. She loves you. She doesn't understand why you're acting the way you are. None of us do. That woman is crazy about you." Horace looked back out the window and then his gaze fell back on Steele. "Steele, I love you like a brother. Please don't do anything to screw up your marriage."

Steele turned his chair to look out the window. He knew Horace was watching him. After a few minutes he turned his chair back so he could look at Horace. "You asked me not to give you a phony answer. The only thing I can say to you right now and I'll not say anything more is this. I've done nothing to violate my love for Randi or my marriage vows. I only wish that I could tell you that Randi hasn't."

A shocked look crossed Horace's face. "I'm sorry, Steele. I'm so sorry. If that's true, I just don't think I could live with that. I'm not sure any man could."

Steele nodded his agreement.

Chapter 33

DEE AND HENRY were cuddled together in a booth at Daisy's Café. It had become one of their favorite places to eat. Henry had originally chosen it because it was on the edge of the city and well off the roads most often frequented by the people in his social circle. He felt confidant that he would never run into a patron of the Magnolia Club or the Country Club at Daisy's. The café was decorated with a lot of antiques from America's rural past. The most distinguished wall hanging was the oversized American flag that hung behind the bar. Beers were always two dollars regardless of the time of day. Daisy only served American beer – no imports ever. On Sunday mornings, Daisy's Café ceased to operate long enough to become a Cowboy Church. Following services each week, it re-opened with the largest buffet in the county.

"When do you think I can meet your daughters?" Dee was anxious to see if they would accept her.

"Dee, Honey. It's far too soon. It's only been a few weeks since Virginia accepted the terms of our divorce. We're going to do this right. "

"What does right mean?" Dee started stroking Henry's leg underneath the table with her hand.

"Dee, the most important part of all of this is to have you accepted by my girls and by Falls City Society. If there is even one hint that you might have been the reason for my divorce, you'll never be accepted. I tell you, Dee, I know this town. They'll brand you with the scarlet letter, and we'll live our entire marriage under a cloud."

Dee put her hands to her breast. "Marriage? Did you say marriage, Henry? Is that a proposal?"

Henry smiled at her. "No you don't. You'll not cheat me out of the opportunity to propose to you in a proper fashion. Everything in due time. For now, let's just be happy. Let's just enjoy our time together. I promise that the time will come for you to meet my daughters. They're going to love you."

"Do you really think so, Henry?"

"I know so. Right now, they're both really angry. We've got to let them adjust. I'm taking them to a counselor. I'll work with the counselor as to when the best time will be to bring you into the picture."

"If you say so. I'm just so anxious to get on with our life together. I want us to be a family."

Henry put his arm around her shoulders and squeezed her. "Me too. Me too."

"Well, if it isn't my favorite love birds." Daisy was standing at their booth. "Just look at the two of you. Hasn't he put a ring on your finger yet?"

Henry and Dee both laughed. "He keeps telling me it's coming."

"Well, as long as you've made her wait, it had better be a big one."

Henry looked at Dee. "It will be. I'm going to want everyone to be able to see it from blocks away. I want folks to know that this beautiful lady belongs to me."

"Can I get you folks anything?"

"No, we've already ordered. We really like your place. The food is excellent and the people here are so friendly."

"You should come see us on Sunday. We have the best and biggest buffet in the county."

"So we hear."

"We also have live music on Sundays. It goes all afternoon."

"Thanks, Daisy. We just might do that very thing."

Daisy turned to walk away when Henry decided to ask her something he'd wanted to know. "Hey Daisy, is that your real name?"

Daisy turned back to look at the two of them. She reached into her pants pocket and brought out a gold rhinestone cigarette case. She put one of the cigarettes in the corner of her mouth and lit it. "Why do you ask?"

"Oh, I don't know. Just curious I guess. We've been coming here so long and so often. Never mind. It's just a question."

"I'll answer your question if you'll answer mine first."

"Fair enough. What do you want to know?"

Daisy took a long drag off her cigarette and then exhaled the smoke. "I know my customers pretty well. They're all pretty much the same. Most of them are working stiffs. Now the two of you don't fit. Look at you, Dee. You've got on a silk dress that most likely came from one of those fancy dress shops down off River Street. And Henry, you're awfully tucked in. My hunch is that suit you're wearing costs more than three monthly payments on my Cadillac out there. What's your story?"

Henry looked at Dee. "We're just a couple of kids in love."

"A couple of escapees from the country club." She took another drag of her cigarette and then turned her head away from them to let the smoke trail off into the air. "Okay. We'll leave it at that, but don't be surprised if I don't ask you for the rest of the story." Daisy turned to walk away.

"What about our deal?"

She turned back. "Oh, my name. Daisy is a pet name my husband gave me. It's just stuck and now everyone calls me Daisy. We even changed the name on this place to Daisy's. My real name is Shirley."

"That's a nice name." Dee smiled.

"Now back to you two. You know there's only one other couple that ever comes in here that looks like they come from your social circle, although they don't dress as fashionably as the two of you. They smell of money. They come in for the fried catfish. They usually come in once a week for lunch and they each have the catfish." Daisy glanced out the window. "In fact, here they come now."

Henry and Dee turned to look out the window. Henry's heart skipped a beat. His first thought was to grab Dee and run for the back door. It was too late. By the time he'd realized there was nothing he could do, Howard and Martha Dexter were standing at their table. "Well, Henry Mudd, what a surprise to see you here. And who is this that you have with you?"

Chapter 34

ALMEDA ALEXANDER DRUMMOND had been sitting at the desk in her sun-room for almost the entire morning. Her singular project this day was to redesign her note card so that it would better reflect the new role in life she was about to assume. Since Horace's election to the Episco-pate was now all but assured, she had made a lengthy list of things that simply had to be accomplished before his consecration.

She had been staring at length at the various proposals the local engraver had given her to consider. Something was just not right. She'd sorted through the proposals over and over again. She'd arranged them on her desk in sequential order from her favorite to her least favorite. Still, something was not right.

As the wife of a Bishop she would be called on to write numerous notes. There would be the many occasions in the lives of the clergy and their families that would mandate a personal note from the Bishop's spouse. But of course, these same occasions would occur in the lives of government and civic leaders throughout the state and then there would be the other Bishops and their families. She must not forget the various executive officers in the national church. She sorted through the proposed designs yet one more time.

She was about to send them all back to the engraver when her eye fell on the problem. Two things in particular stood out. The first was her name. She'd retained her late husband's last name – Alexander. She'd done so to remind society that she was a woman of position. She also wanted to retain his name because of the many doors that it opened for her in Falls City. Her eyes lit up. She was going to be the wife of a Bishop. She no longer needed to retain the name of Alexander. She would tell the engraver to simply record her name on the note cards as Almeda Drummond. She wrinkled her brow. "No," she uttered. "As the wife of the Bishop, my note cards should now read *Mrs. Horace Drummond.*" She wrote that on one of the draft cards. She studied it. Then a thought occurred to her. Priests put a cross at the end of their name. Bishops put a cross in front of their name. Should she put a cross in front of the Mrs.? After all, she was using the name of the Bishop. Yes, of course she should put a cross at the beginning of her name.

Then she looked at the other problem. The engraver had put the Seal of the Diocese on her note cards. She grimaced. "No.... no.... no...that just won't do." The Diocesan Seal made her cards look so clinical. The seal of the Diocese was just too impersonal. Her notes and those of Bishop Drummond needed a more personal touch. Then she realized exactly what needed to be done. She would have the engraver design a logo specifically for Horace. She began drawing some ideas.

After several minutes a large smile crossed her face as she studied her artwork. She had drawn a mitre. Across the base she'd written Horace. That had some possibilities, she thought to herself. Or, she was particularly drawn to the sketch of a crozier. Across the crozier she had written Horace. The length of the crozier had Drummond written on it. Yes. This would give both Horace and her correspondence a much more personal touch. She would instruct his secretary in the Diocese to cease using the Diocesan Seal on Horace's letterhead and use one of her own design instead. This new logo that included Horace's name could also be used on her own note cards as well. Almeda was pleased with her idea. She would take that to the engraver first thing this afternoon. She would have three thousand of them printed up immediately. No. Three thousand would not be enough. She would increase the order to ten thousand. That should last them less than a year.

Almeda then glanced down at her list. She placed a check mark next to the first clergy wives conference she would host. She'd already placed it on her calendar and called the Diocesan Retreat Center to make sure they saved the dates for her. The wives of the clergy in this Diocese needed some help. They all looked so dowdy. At the conference, she'd bring in fashion coordinators to teach them how to dress. She would have a cosmetologist present to teach them about the proper use of feminine products. The one thing she would insist on is that the wives of the priests in this Diocese do something about their weight. If she could maintain her slim body at her age, then women twenty years her junior could do so as well. She would have a nutritionist speak and a personal trainer available to guide them through some critical exercises. She'd also planned to speak to Horace about having the Diocese pay for health club memberships for all the clergy wives.

Now, when it came to the details of social grace, she would teach those sessions herself. She knew of no one more qualified to instruct the clergy wives. Until she married Horace Drummond she had been one of the trainers for the Junior League on this very subject. After she married a black man, they ceased to invite her. She did not want her considerable knowledge on the subject to go to waste. She'd started a book on this very topic. She would now use her lecture notes to the clergy wives to complete that work. God only knows that it was much needed. She could not believe how little most people knew about these finer points of being a proper hostess.

She picked up her list. Her interior decorator would be here tomorrow with some fabric samples. Even though they would need to get a town house in Savannah, they would still maintain their home in Falls City. Once they'd chosen a dwelling in Savannah, she'd have a decorator work with her to make sure that it was a home suitable for the Bishop. She did not want to overuse purple coverings in their home, but she certainly wanted to use enough so that their guests would know they were in the Bishop's residence. Or should she call it a palace? Bishops of old lived in palaces. Perhaps she should have that added to her note cards above the address. They could have their residential palace in Savannah and their summer palace in Falls City. She made herself a note. **+Mrs. Horace Drummond—The Bishop's Summer Palace – Falls City, Georgia.** Then she scribbled, **+Mrs. Horace Drummond – The Bishop's Residential Palace – Savannah, Georgia.** She would give these notes to the engraver first thing in the morning. Anyway, her decorator would be bringing some purple fabrics for her to consider for their house. She'd start with the living room and dining room.

"Speaking of fabrics..." Almeda muttered. She hurried up the stairs to her dressing room and threw open the closet doors. She began sorting through the various new dresses she'd purchased for herself. All of them were tasteful and befitting the wife of a Bishop. She planned to go with Horace on all his visitations to the various congregations in the Diocese. She would save all her new purple dresses for those occasions. She opened her wall vault. She pulled out the two velvet boxes. She'd had her jeweler design two identical gold crosses with large gold crowns. The one for Horace was larger than hers and had one large amethyst stone in the center of the cross. Her cross was identical to his, only smaller. She had placed three smaller amethyst stones on her cross. She would wear her purple cross and her purple dresses on visitations and other church affairs she attended with Horace. That way every person that cast their eyes on her would know that she was the Bishop's wife.

She picked up a stack of shirt boxes from the floor. She opened one of them. Horace had been making noises about not wearing a purple shirt. She simply would not hear of it. She'd had the local tailor make him a dozen of these shirts. She'd present them to him as a gift. He wouldn't be able to deny her gift. "Horace Drummond, you're going to be the Bishop of this Diocese, and you're going to look like one."

Almeda reached into the back of her closet. She pulled out a single purple dress of brocade fabric. Gold trim had been used around the neck, bodice and sleeves. She unzipped the plastic garment bag and pulled the dress out so she could admire it. She had this dress specifically designed by an exclusive dressmaker up in Atlanta. This is the dress that she would wear when she met the Queen of England. Every ten years the Bishops and their wives attended Lambeth Conference in England. Invariably, the Queen would hold a tea party for them. Almeda walked to the full-length mirror in her dressing closet. She held the dress in front of her and practiced a curtsy. She was pleased with her reflection. She smiled, "Who would have ever thought? I'm going to meet the Queen." Almeda carefully placed the dress back in the garment bag and returned to her desk.

She once again examined her list. There was only one thing left to decide and with this she would have her way as well. She'd not have Horace wearing one of those mitres. She'd yet to see a Bishop that looked good in one. He could wear a cope if he wanted, but not the hat. Every Bishop she'd ever seen wearing one looked just like they were wearing one of those *Dunce Caps* they used to put on the dumb kids in her country school. She'd not be humiliated by having her husband parade around in a *Dunce Cap*.

She opened the catalog of clergy vestments she kept in her desk drawer. "Now, that's what you should wear all the time." She pointed to a red robe with a large white alb over it. She read the description. It was called a Rochet and Chimere. She read that it finds its origin in the House of Lords in the English Parliament. "That's it. That's what you're going to wear, Bishop Drummond. You are going to wear robes befitting a member of the House of Lords."

Almeda put the catalog back in the drawer. She sat staring out the window. She was so pleased with her newest lot in life. She would be married to a Bishop. "My Lord Bishop," she uttered. She was so happy. "My Lord Bishop. Oh, I do like the way that sounds." Then the thought hit her. If Horace could be properly addressed as My Lord Bishop, did that mean she should insist the clergy and their wives address her as *My Lady?* She thought about it.—*Lady Drummond. "Ladies and Gentlemen, it is my distinct pleasure to present to you the Lord Bishop of Savannah and his lovely...no, his beautiful wife. Will you please stand to receive Lord and Lady Drummond?"* Almeda smiled. Yes, she would instruct the clergy and their wives to so address her.

Chapter 35

"GIRL, YOU'RE BRINGING me down. Now get dressed and let's go out on the town." Alicia surveyed Virginia's living room. "Look at this place, Virginia. This is a dump. It would help if you'd unpack these boxes and take out the trash. Do you even know how to wash dishes, Virginia?"

"Shady used to do all that for me."

"Well, you didn't get Shady in the divorce so you're going to have to learn to take care of yourself."

"You're so mean to me. I thought you were my friend."

"I am your friend, Virginia. I'm probably the only friend you have left in all of Falls City. Now go clean yourself up and let's go out on the town. "

"And do what?"

"Well, for starters, let's see if we can't get ourselves picked up by a couple of tall, dark and handsome men."

"Where am I going to go? Everyone knows me. They'll all talk about me."

"Virginia, what planet do you live on? This town is already talking about you, so, to hell with them. Let's get out there and really give them something to talk about."

Virginia sat looking around her tiny little house. "Can you believe this is the best I can do? Henry's not giving me enough money to get anything better."

"Girl, with all that Henry had on you you're damn lucky to have this place. At least you have a separate bedroom for your daughters so they can sleep over when they visit."

"Do you think they're really going to want to? I mean…they have their own rooms and everything with Henry."

"Virginia, your daughters love you. They're going to get over all this. You're all going to get through this. Just give it some time."

Alicia reached into her purse and brought out a joint. She sang, "Look what I have!"

Virginia lit up. "Give me. Please. Please. Pretty please with sugar on it."

Alicia drew the marijuana deep into her lungs and then passed it to Virginia. "Oh, that's good stuff."

"Primo. Now, put on your party dress. There are men in this town waiting on us, and they're in for a treat."

The Atlantic Grill sits on Macon Road just blocks from the mansions on River Street. It's a favorite hangout for the church-going social set in Falls City. Wednesday nights are particularly popular. Following Wednesday night church and programs, they all drive directly to The Atlantic Grill. The Grill has a fairly respectable wine list so most folks gather in the bar before going to their tables. The crowd at the bar is a mixture of Presbyterians, Methodists, and Episcopalians, with a few of the more progressive Baptists thrown in. It's also a favorite for out of town salesmen.

Alicia had a difficult time finding a place to park her car in the parking lot so she ended up parking on the street a good block from the restaurant. "This place is really hopping tonight."

"Oh, no." Virginia complained.

"What?"

"It's Wednesday night. The place is going to be filled with church people. There's bound to be a bunch of people from First Church in there. Let's go somewhere else."

"No, Virginia. Screw them. You're a divorced woman. Now hold your head high and let's go in there and have a good time." Alicia handed Virginia a silver flask. "Here, swallow some of this. It'll give you the courage you need."

"I'm already high."

"Then let's go in there and get drunk. Come on, men are waiting."

To Virginia's surprise, when they walked into the bar, all eyes did not turn to look at her. People were engaged in conversation. No one even looked her direction. They spotted two seats at the bar. Virginia and Alicia walked directly to them. Once they'd ordered their drinks, Virginia dared to use the mirror behind the bar to look around. She did recognize a few familiar faces, but they were not people that she and Henry socialized with. She didn't even know their names. She turned her barstool so that she could look into the dining room. There were Elmer and Judith Idle. They were sitting in a booth. They both had their eyes closed. Judith was holding her hands palms up. Obviously she was blessing the food they'd just been served. Virginia resolved not to look that direction again.

"Can we buy you ladies a drink?"

Virginia smiled at the two men in airline uniforms. "Are you gentlemen pilots?"

"I'm a pilot, Mark here wishes he was."

"Don't pay any attention to him. Yes, we're both pilots."

Alicia beamed. "For what airlines?"

"We fly charters. We brought four guys up here from Jacksonville to play golf."

"Why Falls City? I mean, we've only got a couple of golf courses."

"Let's just say that's what they told their wives. They're on a golf outing." The two men winked at each other.

"Now, what are you ladies drinking?"

Virginia remembered thinking the pilot that favored her was quite handsome. He had a beautiful smile. She remembered that his teeth were really white. The next thing she remembered was the sound of a police siren outside her window. She woke, rubbed her eyes and looked around. At first, she didn't recognize anything. She sat up on the bed. It was then she realized she was in a hotel room. She got up and walked to the bathroom. There was no one there. She was alone in the room. She looked out the window. She was in the Confederate Hotel right in the heart of downtown Falls City. She tried to shake the cobwebs out of her head. Then she saw the condom wrapper on the table beside the bed. There was an envelope propped up next to the lamp.

She opened it. There were three one hundred dollar bills in it wrapped in a note. She read the note. "*Thanks for a great evening. You're actually quite good at your job. We never discussed a price. I hope this covers it.* "

Virginia sat down on the side of the bed. She realized that the pilot had thought she was a hooker. She ran for the shower. She washed herself over and over again. She still didn't feel clean. She dressed and rode the elevator down to the lobby. The only people in sight were the desk clerk and the bellman. The bellman gave her a broad smile. Virginia hurried out onto the main street. Then, just as she was coming out of the hotel, she ran directly into Henry. They stopped and looked at each other. Henry glanced back over her shoulder towards the hotel. Then, with words that only added to her humiliation, he sneered at her. "Virginia. Are you working the hotels now?"

Chapter 36

"I TELL YOU, Mary Alice, we saw him for ourselves. Howard and I went out to Daisy's Café for lunch."

"Where? What on earth is Daisy's Café?"

Mary Alice Smythe and Martha Dexter had agreed to meet at *The Doll House* on Camellia Avenue for lunch. The Doll House was well named. It was actually a small one-bedroom cottage that sat just a half block below the Women's Club and Gardens. At one time, a reclusive spinster had lived in the cottage. Her only companion was a grey cat. No one knew much about her. She kept to herself her entire life. When she died, the local authorities were completely unable to find any relatives to manage her final arrangements. She did leave a will, which included instructions for her burial and the distribution of her limited assets to the local animal society. She included a provision that they provide for her cat and agree never to euthanize her. The proceeds from the sale of her house and possessions were to go to the animal society as well.

The house and contents were placed up for sale and two young men bought the entire package. When they began going through the boxes in the house, they discovered dozens of porcelain dolls. The woman had made all of them. The two young men converted the woman's cottage into a teahouse. They placed the dolls strategically about the living room and named their new venture *The Doll House*.

Since there was limited seating in the living room, reservations were required several days in advance. Martha Dexter and Mary Alice Smythe were now dining on finger sandwiches and sipping hot tea.

"Daisy's Café has the best fried catfish in the county. My Howard discovered it several years ago when he went dove hunting with some men from his office."

Where is it located?"

"Oh, it's on the edge of town. You've probably driven past it hundreds of times but never even given it notice. It's just not the kind of place you and Gordon would have wanted to stop. It appeals primarily to the country folk. It has a western theme. But Howard just loved the way they did the catfish. We've been going there once a week for lunch. I've never eaten anything else there."

"So you saw Henry Mudd out there?"

"We did. We walked in and there he was sitting in a booth talking to Daisy."

"Daisy?"

"Yes, she owns the place. I'm not sure I know if that's her real name or a nickname. Anyway, Henry had his arm wrapped around this gorgeous young woman. He appeared to be really taken back to see us. He turned as white as a Klan Sheet."

The two women chuckled. "Did he introduce you to the woman?"

One of the owners of The Doll House arrived with some more hot water and fresh tea bags. "He seems awfully light in his loafers, don't you think?"

Martha gave the young man a long stare as he walked away. "I'm pretty sure that both of them are as queer as a three legged dog. Who else would think of turning this little cottage into a teahouse? Just look around. Look at the way they've decorated it. I don't think there's any doubt about it."

"Did Henry introduce you to the woman?"

"He did. He said her name was Delilah. Only he kept calling her Dee. He said her last name, but I don't recall it right now."

"What did he tell you about her?"

"He didn't volunteer much, but Howard and I both concluded that they were lovers. They were just awfully familiar with each other."

"Did he tell you anything about her?"

"Not really. I asked several questions, but he wasn't very forthcoming."

"So do you think it's been going on for a long time?"

"Howard thought so and I agree with him. I'll just bet you that hussy is the reason for his divorce from Virginia."

"Poor Virginia. We've just got to reach out to her. I think this has all been so humiliating for her. What do you think we can do for her?"

"I don't know. She's really dropped out of sight. I haven't seen her in church in months. She's given up her Altar Guild work and all her volunteer duties in the community."

"Well, wouldn't you if you'd discovered that your husband was divorcing you so he could marry his lover?"

"Now Mary Alice, in all fairness, we don't know that. I mean, sure we saw him with that woman, but he didn't say anything about marriage."

"He didn't have to." Mary Alice shook her head. "I just never thought that Henry Mudd was the type of man that would do such a thing. Poor Virginia. Poor, poor Virginia. We've just got to do something for her."

The waiter returned with a small saucer of cookies. "Ladies, these are fresh baked. We just brought them out of the oven. Please enjoy them with our compliments."

Martha Dexter immediately grabbed one of the cookies and started chewing it with an open mouth. "I heard that she's living in a tiny little house over near the carpet mill."

Mary Alice was using her own napkin to deflect the crumbs coming at her out of Martha's mouth. "Martha, please. Chew with your mouth shut."

"Oh, Mary Alice, you know these teeth won't allow me to do that."

"Well, then, don't talk with your mouth full. It seems to me we've had this conversation before."

Martha took another bite of her cookie and tried to force herself to chew with a closed mouth. She bit her lower lip and flinched. "I just can't do it."

"Have you ever thought about seeing an orthodontist?"

"Mary Alice, you know who I'm married to. Howard Dexter is not about to pay for anything that looks like a luxury. He would consider having my teeth corrected an unnecessary expense."

"Well, I think I'd insist."

"And that's because you don't really know my Howard. If he could figure out a way to limit the amount of bath water I run in my tub, he'd do it."

"I just don't know how you've put up with his…well, let's just call it frugality."

"He's as tight as they come. I know that and you know it. But I love him."

"Back to Virginia. Maybe we should go by and see her."

"I think that's a good idea, but I think first I'm going to make a call on Henry Mudd."

"Why would you want to do that?"

"I've known him since he was a little boy." Mary Alice stiffened in her seat. "His momma and daddy are gone, but I'm still here. Someone needs to remind him of just who he is and that we expect more out of him then this. I'm going to give him a piece of my mind. If I could, I'd turn him over my knee and spank him. Yes, I think that's the first thing we should do. I need to remind him that adultery is a sin. He should be ashamed of himself. It just makes me so mad to think of him sneaking around on that sweet wife of his. I just can't believe that he would do this to our precious Virginia and those beautiful little girls. I'll swear. I just don't know what he was thinking. I may spank him anyway."

"I'll go with you."

"Would you?"

"I sure will. Let's go by his office right now and demand that he see us."

One of the young men brought them their check. Martha Dexter picked it up and studied it. "Now, Mary Alice, you had the black tea. That was twenty-five cents more than the house tea that I had. Let me see, with tax that means you owe twenty-six, no make that twenty-seven cents more than I do. I'll subtract that amount from my half of the check."

Chapter 37

"HAVE YOU LOOKED out there?" Horace Drummond walked into the sacristy with a big smile on his face.

Steele returned his smile and nodded. Just then Mrs. Gordon Smythe hurried into the priest's sacristy. "Misturh Austin, I've got to get some more wine out of the lock up. We prepared the altar for no more than one hundred people. There must be five or six hundred out there. We simply must reset the service."

Horace grinned. "I have to hand it to you, Steele. I just didn't expect this kind of response."

Steele finished putting on his preaching stole. "Quite frankly, neither did I. I figured maybe half this many."

Ginnifer Graystone added, "I think it's really exciting."

"You realize that about a third of the folks out there have black faces."

"I told Josiah to invite his congregation if he wanted. Did you see him?"

"Yes, and Rubidoux is wearing a hat big enough to land a small aircraft on."

"She does have an interesting taste in clothing, but Josiah seems to approve."

"Oh, Steele, it's not just her. All of my people dress extravagantly at Easter. This was one of the holidays that slaves did not have to work, so the custom of dressing up for Easter is our way to remember that. I'm sure that custom predates the Easter Parade down Fifth Avenue."

"I'm not so sure I knew that, Horace. Thanks for telling me."

Horace grinned. 'I believe all the kids from Noah's House are out there as well. They've brought a lot of their friends with them."

"That's just great."

"I'm not so sure. You have all those black folks dressed in their many colors and the gay and lesbian crowd that are rather colorful in themselves. The only thing missing is a large rainbow flag over the front door. I don't know if we're going to have a church service or a Pride Parade. Let's just hope the Klan doesn't get wind of what's going on over here tonight."

Ginnifer added, "I talked to several of the kids from Rainbow House before the service. They invited a lot of their friends to come with them tonight. I'll see you both at the back of the church."

After she left, Steele whispered in Horace's ear. "Have you heard the gossip?"

Horace nodded. "It's everywhere you go. It's almost like Henry and Virginia's divorce is the first one to ever occur."

"I know."

"The speculation is off the charts. I've heard everything from *he has a girlfriend* to *she was starring in porno films*."

Steele nodded. "I think the most ridiculous accusation yet is that they were caught up in a wife swapping club."

"You do know that there are some rumors of that very thing going on with one of the couples in this parish."

"No."

"Do you know the Adams?"

"Know them? Randi and I have been in their home several times. They seem like awfully nice people to me."

"That may be, but I have it on pretty good authority that they're engaged in wife swapping."

"I just don't want to believe that. They're so nice. In fact they've been extra nice to us."

A mischievous smile spread across Horace's face. "Oh, and you don't suppose that had anything to do with the fact that the two of you are not all that hard to look at?"

"I'm sorry, Horace. That's all gossip and until I have proof, I refuse to believe it."

"Well, brother, in this case you need to believe it. I just don't know if Virginia and Henry are involved in it."

Steele answered Horace firmly. "I can guarantee you that Henry was not involved in anything like that. He's just not the type. He is an all around decent man."

Horace gave Steele a long look. "But you aren't so sure about Virginia? Interesting."

Steele shrugged.

"How do you plan to deal with all the gossip about Henry and Virginia? It's putting a real black eye on First Church in this community. After all, he's been on the Vestry and she is so prominent socially."

"I plan to meet it head on. And I plan to start with my sermon this very night."

"Well, I can hardly wait to hear that sermon."

Just then the Verger entered. "We've got a standing room only crowd, Father Austin. Are you ready?"

Steele looked at Horace. "Let's go celebrate the resurrection."

They followed the Verger to the door. A thurifer, crucifer, and two torchbearers were waiting on them. The timpani began to sound a low roll growing slightly louder. Horace announced, "Christ is risen."

The people responded. "He is risen, indeed."

The timpani grew louder. Horace announced again even louder. "Christ is risen."

The people responded more loudly. "He is risen, indeed."

The timpani now filled the church with sound. Horace shouted, "Christ is risen."

The people shouted even more loudly, "He is risen, indeed."

Then the timpani, organ and bass ensemble all sounded a great fanfare as the procession moved down the center aisle. The choir from Josiah's church was not used to a formal procession behind a cross and incense, but they all had broad smiles on their faces. Once the procession reached the front of the church and Horace had blessed the altar with the incense, the choir began singing "O Happy Day." They swayed and clapped their hands. The people in the congregation were caught up in the moment and soon they too were clapping their hands.

Horace leaned over and whispered to Steele. "Who would have ever thought this could happen at First Church?"

Then it was time for Steele's sermon. "I want to welcome all of you to this Easter celebration. I want to especially welcome the choir from the Creekwood Christian Church. I want to thank my friend, The Reverend Josiah Williams and his wife Rubidoux for worshipping with us tonight. I thank him for loaning us this fine choir. And we welcome all the members of his congregation and all our guests to this service this night. When it comes time for communion, I want you to know that all who seek our Lord Jesus Christ are welcome at the communion rail.

I also want you to note that this may be the last time that Doctor Drummond celebrates the Mass in this parish as a priest. God willing, next Saturday he will be elected Bishop of this Diocese." Steele's words were met with enthusiastic applause.

"Now, I don't want to shock any of you, but I need to tell you some things about the Church of Jesus Christ. First, I need to tell you that that the Church is filled with hypocrites. You heard me right. The Church has hypocrites in it. There are men and women in the Church that take vows to stay faithful to one another until death parts them, but one or both of them fail to keep that vow and their marriage often ends in divorce. Church leaders get caught in sexual scandals. Church officers are caught stealing from the Church. In the words of the Prayer Book, we all do those things we ought not do and we leave undone those things we ought to do. That makes us all sinners or as some prefer to call us – hypocrites."

The congregation chuckled and nodded their heads in agreement. "Now, my fellow hypocrites, I welcome you to the empty tomb of Jesus. He died and rose again with the full knowledge that we all will continue to sin. That's not permission." Again the congregation chuckled. "It's just a dose of reality. We strive to be better. As the blessed apostle reminds us, we have not yet attained the prize, but we continue the race."

Steele stopped to look out at the congregation that was standing along the walls of the church and spilling out into the narthex. "We live in a world in which many folks have given up on the Church. They've given up on us precisely because we fail to be perfect. But my friends, God uses imperfect people because there are no perfect ones available. The Bible is filled with hypocrites who became powerful instruments for God. Have you forgotten Noah the drunk or Moses the murderer? Have you forgotten that David was an adulterer and murderer? Or that Peter denied Jesus three times? Today's critics would label all of them hypocrites. They were sinners that God used to achieve his purposes on earth. And, my fellow hypocrites, this same God can use every one of us for his purposes." That statement was met with applause and several *Amens*.

"I don't have to remind you that some of the chapters in the Church's history are dark. There are terrible things that Christians have done to others and to one another in the name of their religion. The list could be lengthy if I chose to recite it. But do we give up on education, when educational practices in times gone by were often cruel?"

To Steele's surprise, the congregation shouted, "No!"

"Do we give up on medicine, when the practices of medicine in days gone by were barbaric at best?"

"No!" The people shouted.

"And what of government? Some of the most unspeakable horrors in history have been unleashed on humanity by the very government that was supposed to protect us. Do we give up?"

"No!" The crowd responded.

"So where do we see the evidence of the resurrected Christ in the Church? We see him present around the world in the poorest of the poor who receive food, housing, and medical care by the very Church some have given up on."

"Amen" was shouted from the pews.

"And right here in Falls City this very congregation operates a Soup Kitchen, a Free Medical Clinic, and provides housing for children that have been rejected by their very own families. Do we give up on the Church because the people doing these good things are less than perfect?"

"No!"

"Do we give up because these good things are being done by people who on occasion fail to live up to the very ideals they profess?"

"No!" Came the loudest shout of the evening.

"My brothers and sisters, if you would see Jesus, look at all the good He's able to do with all of us hypocrites. He works through us not because we are sin free, but he works through us knowing that we are not."

More people shouted *Amen*. And then to his complete surprise, the congregation applauded.

"Sick people belong in hospitals. The Church is such a hospital. It is a hospital for sinners. Sinners come here seeking to be healed and forgiven for things done and left undone. Here the Risen Christ welcomes us. He forgives us. And then He sends us out into the world to do better. Yes, we fail. But the Church also succeeds. If we would see Jesus then let's focus on the good that He is able to do through imperfect people. Forgive one another for our failings just as he forgives us."

Steele was interrupted yet one more time with applause.

"I want to conclude my remarks by reciting a prayer that is attributed to a Negro slave. I know that it is not politically correct. However, it's the way the way that saintly woman referred to herself. Here is her prayer. *Lord, I know that I'm not all I'm supposed to be. And Lord, I know that I'm not yet what I'm gonna be. But, Lord, I sure thank you that I'm not what I used to be.*"

With that the congregation rose to their feet and gave Steele's sermon a standing ovation. Then the choir began to sing – *The stone is rolled away – The soldiers ran away – The body has gone away – Jesus – oh, Jesus – is risen today.*"

Steele sank into his seat next to the altar. He was drained. He'd never received that kind of response to one of his sermons. He looked out at the congregation. It was a rainbow of colors, ages, and sexuality. The poor and the rich were sitting next to one another. The old and the young, black and white, gay and straight all gathered in one house of worship. They had all come to this place with one purpose in mind. They were here to celebrate the resurrection of Jesus. Then he looked to the altar. Seated behind it was a black priest, his dear friend that he believed was about to be elected a Bishop. Seated next to him was a white woman priest. Tears clouded Steele's eyes as he remembered the words of Jesus. *In my Father's house there are many rooms."* This was the Church of Jesus Christ. In spite of the Elmer and Judith Idles, the Ned Boones, and the Friar Means that want to treat it as their personal plaything, tonight, he was able to see the Church as God sees it. He closed his eyes and offered a prayer of gratitude.

Chapter **38**

THE CONVENTION FOR the electing of a Bishop Coadjutor for the Diocese of Savannah was being held in the Cathedral in the city of Savannah, Georgia. The Right Reverend Rufus Petersen, the current Diocesan Bishop, presided over the election process. Every priest in the Diocese in good standing could vote for the selection of a new bishop. Every congregation in the Diocese had elected delegates to attend the convention. Each parish, regardless of size, was assured of two lay delegates. Parishes with more than five hundred members could send four delegates. The four lay delegates from First Church in Falls City were Elmer and Judith Idle, Ned Boone, and the current Junior Warden, Gary Hendricks.

Bishop Petersen led the gathered delegates in an opening celebration of the Holy Eucharist. During his sermon, he recited several notable achievements he believed the Diocese had enjoyed during his Episcopate. He also apologized to the Diocese for his many shortcomings and begged their forgiveness. For all the good that had been accomplished, he asked the delegates to give the credit and glory to God.

When the convention reconvened for the election, the Bishop announced that he had engaged in much deliberation and prayer regarding the election process. He had also had extended conversations with Canon Vernon and the nominating committee. They had decided that the election of his successor would be under the complete guidance of the Holy Spirit. He and the nominating committee had agreed that the results of each ballot would not be posted until a bishop had been elected. The convention would sing a hymn and offer a prayer before each ballot was cast. Once the ballots had been cast, the convention would once again become a convention devoted to prayer and the singing of hymns. The nominating committee would only report whether or not there had been an election. If no election was achieved on a given ballot, the convention would continue the process until such time as a bishop is elected.

"I think we should object to that, Father Austin." Ned Boone leaned forward in the pew that had been designated for the clergy and convention delegates from First Church.

Steele leaned forward so he could see him. "Why?"

"That just doesn't seem right. I think we should know who the convention favors after each ballot."

Steele shrugged his shoulders. "I don't know what we can do about it. The Bishop is the presiding officer and the nominating committee is in charge of the process."

"Don't you agree, Elmer? I think we should stand up and raise an objection."

Elmer pursed his lips. "Ned, I agree with your sentiment, but I think Father Austin is correct. There isn't anything that we can do about it. The decision has been made."

Judith beamed. "Oh, I think it's exciting. We're all going to be completely under the guidance of the Holy Spirit." She lifted her hands, shut her eyes and begin to mumble prayers.

"Well, if you all say so, but I just want to go on record that I don't like it." Ned looked at Gary. "What do you think?"

"I don't have a legal opinion on the matter. I'm not sure what the Canons have to say about it." Gary looked down the pew at Steele. "Where's Doctor Drummond?"

"The nominating committee asked all the nominees to remain in their homes. The head teller is supposed to call the candidate that has been elected to gain their consent to the election and then report that to the Bishop for announcement."

"Aren't you the head teller, Elmer?" Ned Boone grinned.

Elmer beamed. "I am. Just think. Sometime in the next few hours I'm going to be calling Horace Drummond and informing him that he is now the Bishop of the Diocese of Savannah. Isn't that exciting? A priest of First Church will become the Bishop of this Diocese."

Ned smiled. "It's so exciting. This is a proud day for First Church and we all get to be a part of it."

The ballots were distributed and the entire First Church Delegation marked their ballots for Horace Drummond. They handed them to Steele, who was sitting at the end of the pew, to hand to the tellers collecting them. Elmer made a point of handing his ballot to Steele last. He placed it on top of the stack. He left it unfolded. He wanted to make sure that Steele saw that he'd marked his ballot for Horace Drummond. "Okay, wish First Church luck. I've got to go count the ballots."

"Now, Elmer. Luck has nothing to do with this. It's all up to the Holy Spirit." Judith chastised her husband.

"Yes, Darling. As usual, you're right."

The Bishop had the congregation stand to sing two hymns while the ballots were being counted. They then sang a third and were halfway through the fourth hymn when Elmer Idle and the other tellers reappeared. Elmer handed the Bishop a note. The Bishop opened the note and motioned for the organist to stop playing. "My brothers and sisters, the tellers have just informed me that on the first ballot we have failed to elect a bishop. Will you please kneel for prayers before we receive a second ballot?"

This process was repeated a second, third, and fourth time. The convention was getting restless. Ned Boone went to the microphone. "Right Reverend, Sir. I believe it would be advantageous for the delegates to be able to see the number of votes being cast for each candidate. I believe that would expedite the election process."

"Mister Boone from First Church, isn't it?" The Bishop remained seated.

"Yes, sir."

"That's exactly what we are trying to avoid. We don't want to rush through this election. We don't want it to be a political process. We are trusting completely in the guidance of the Holy Spirit. I am prepared to stay here all night if that's how long it takes for us to discern the will of God in the selection of our next Bishop. Therefore, in light of the procedure we are using, I must rule your request as being out of order."

"Then I would like to register an objection."

"Thank you, Mister Boone. Please be seated. Your objection is duly noted."

When Elmer reappeared with the results of the fifth ballot, he winked at Jim Vernon. Canon Jim Vernon, who was sitting next to the Bishop, nodded at Elmer. The Canon then whispered in the Bishop's ear.

"My Brothers and Sisters, my good Canon here has reminded me that we've been at prayer for a considerable time now. After we take this next ballot, I am going to declare a twenty-minute recess. Please take advantage of this time to take care of your physical needs and to stretch your legs."

Elmer went into the Dean's office in the Cathedral and shut the door behind him. He picked up the telephone that was designated for him to use to inform the nominee that he'd been elected Bishop. He called Horace Drummond. When the telephone rang, Almeda stood and ran toward it. She just knew that Horace had been elected. "Oh, Horace. I'm so excited. You've just been elected a Bishop."

Horace's hand was shaking. "He picked up the receiver and put it to his ear. This is Horace Drummond."

"Dr. Drummond, this is Elmer Idle. I'm calling from the convention."

Horace looked at Almeda and smiled. Almeda began dancing around the room.

"Yes, Elmer."

"Horace. I'm afraid I have some bad news." Horace snapped his fingers. Almeda turned to look at him. He shook his head. Almeda sank into a nearby chair. Disappointment ran through her.

"I assume that you mean I wasn't elected."

"No one has been elected just yet."

"Then why are you calling me?"

"I'm hoping I can save you some embarrassment. I'm also hoping I can save First Church some embarrassment. I'm not supposed to be making this call, but I just felt like I had to let you know."

"Know what?"

"Horace, you're just not getting very many votes."

"That's disappointing."

"In fact, you're so far behind the other three candidates that I'm glad they're not publishing the votes. It would be so embarrassing for you and for First Church."

"Oh, I guess I'm not really all that surprised. What do you think I should do?"

"Frankly, I think you should withdraw."

Horace looked at the disappointment on Almeda's face. He certainly didn't want to add humiliation to it. "You're right. If I don't have any support, then the right thing to do is to withdraw. Please inform the Bishop."

"I'm so sorry, Horace. This is not the call I wanted to make. I was looking forward to making a completely different call."

"I know you were. I appreciate that."

"Horace, this call is highly irregular."

"I know, but I appreciate your thoughtfulness."

Elmer Idle reported the results of the sixth ballot to the Bishop. The delegates were once again informed that they'd failed to elect. Then Elmer whispered in the Bishop's ear. The Bishop gave Elmer a surprised look. "Are you sure?"

Elmer nodded.

"I need to advise the delegates that we have just been informed that The Reverend Doctor Horace Drummond has asked that his name be removed from any further consideration. There was an audible gasp from the delegates. Confused looks were exchanged between the several delegates. "Please mark your ballots removing Doctor Drummond from any further consideration."

Steele and the First Church delegation sat in quiet disbelief. Only Steele and Ginnifer Graystone, however, felt genuine disappointment.

As Elmer turned from the Bishop, he looked at Jim Vernon and winked. The Canon struggled to keep his smile of satisfaction from spreading completely across his face.

On the seventh ballot, The Reverend Canon Sean Evans was elected as Bishop Coadjutor of the Episcopal Diocese of Savannah.

As per the custom at Electing Conventions throughout the Episcopal Church, the congregation then stood and sang a hymn giving God credit for their choice of a Bishop.

Steele Austin could not get to a telephone fast enough. "Horace, why did you withdraw?"

"I got a call from Elmer Idle. He told me he wanted to save me from embarrassment."

"What kind of embarrassment?"

"Steele, he knew he wasn't supposed to tell me, but he said that I simply wasn't getting very many votes. He told me that I was so far behind the other three candidates that it could prove humiliating when the votes are reported in the Diocesan newspaper."

Something just didn't feel right to Steele. "Horace, I'm not sure that phone call should've been made. I think Elmer was totally out of line."

"I know, Steele. But I appreciate it. He was right to call me. There's no reason to have insult added to injury. He did the right thing."

"If you say so. I'll come by when I get back to Falls City. We'll have a drink and toast our continued ministry together at First Church."

Steele was walking to his car in the Cathedral parking lot when he heard Bishop Petersen calling to him. The Bishop was standing at his Cadillac in the space reserved for his car. Steele walked up to him. "Father Austin, why did Horace Drummond withdraw?"

"I just telephoned him and asked him that very thing. He said that he'd gotten a call from the head teller advising him that he wasn't receiving very many votes."

"I smell a skunk." The Bishop spit the words.

"What?"

"Let me show you something. I have the teller sheets right here for each ballot." The Bishop showed Steele the results. From the very first ballot the convention was equally divided between Horace and Sean Evans. On the sixth ballot Horace was actually elected in the clergy house. He was certain to be elected on the very next ballot in the lay house. But he withdrew from the process. That allowed Sean Evans to be elected on the seventh ballot."

Steele stared at the sheets. Anger rose up inside him. He glared at the Bishop. "Isn't there something that we can do about this?"

The Bishop shook his head. "Canon Evans has to get the approval of a majority of the Standing Committees in each Diocese. I suppose Horace could advise the Standing Committees in the hope that they might overturn the election. I'd be happy to write a letter on his behalf myself. My hunch is that Horace Drummond won't do that."

Steele agreed. "He's just not that kind of guy. He'll ride quietly into the night before he'll be a part of exposing this scandal. But I need to tell him."

"And what about Elmer Idle?"

"I plan to tell everyone I know exactly what he's done. Let's just say I don't know how to be as gracious as Horace."

"Steele, could I give you a piece of advice?"

"Of course."

"These results are going to be published in the Diocesan Paper. They will be in every household in the Diocese in two weeks. Let the process work. Let the people find out for themselves just what happened. The people at First Church and in this Diocese that have an ethical code will isolate Elmer Idle. There's no need for you to do it."

Steele nodded. "But I need to tell Horace."

"I don't think anyone should tell him but you."

The Bishop turned to get into his car. "Steele, one more piece of advice from a tired old man who has been forced to learn most of his lessons in life the hard way."

"I'm listening."

"There's so much truth to the old adage about lying down with pigs. There's absolutely no way to do it without getting up splattered with mud. And it's ever so difficult to get that smell off you."

Chapter 39

SHE WAS SWEATING profusely. She had to keep mopping her upper lip and forehead with a tissue. She had to remove her hands from the steering wheel of the car from time to time and wipe them on her skirt. Virginia Mudd knew she really wanted to give this a try. She'd heard about this group. Her research had caused her to draw the conclusion that she wanted to do it in a group where no one would know her. She had driven for over an hour to Madison, Georgia. She pulled her car up in front of the place they were to meet. She started to turn off the engine, but her shaking hands wouldn't allow her to do it. She put her car in gear and pulled out of her parking space.

Virginia was out of control. She knew she was out of control. She had completely ruined her life. She felt most guilty about her daughters. Neither of them wanted to be around her. They refused to return her phone calls. When they were supposed to be with her, they refused to go. They both gave her sullen, angry looks. They spoke so disrespectfully to her. She knew they blamed her for ruining their perfect lives.

Her oldest daughter was dressing like a slut. She had now pierced her nose. She was running with a wild crowd from the public school. She'd given up all her friends at First Church School. She couldn't believe her youngest. She just kept getting fatter and fatter. She spent all her after school time stretched out on the couch in front of the television — eating continually. The headmaster had told Henry that if both their daughter's grades didn't improve, he was going to have to remove them from the school.

Virginia hadn't been back to church in so long. She just couldn't subject herself to the judgmental looks she knew she would receive. She'd asked to be placed on the inactive lists of all the church and community service groups that used to nurture her. Even Alicia had distanced herself. She'd have to telephone her several times before she'd return her call. One afternoon she went by Alicia's house and rang the doorbell. She knew that Alicia was there. Her car was in the driveway, but Alicia failed to answer the door. When she was able to talk with Alicia, she gave her the hardest looks. Her words were cold and without any feeling. "Virginia, you are really messed up. You need to get some help. I'm not going to let you bring me down with you."

Virginia reached the edge of town. She made a u-turn. She looked at her watch. The event was scheduled to begin at seven o'clock. It was now 7:15. She was late. Maybe she should just wait until the next time. She drove past the front of the building one more time. There were no parking places. She turned the corner and found a place to park. The sweat began streaming down her face. She looked in the mirror. After dabbing her face with a tissue she reapplied her makeup. "I don't suppose for something like this it matters whether or not you're on time." She was nervous but pleased that her hands were no longer shaking. She so wanted to do this. From the time she'd heard about these groups she'd wanted to be a part of one. She kept telling herself she owed it to herself to do it. She opened the door and got out. She walked to the corner and then the half block down to the meeting place. Once again, she froze. She was now almost thirty minutes late. Maybe she should postpone and give it a try another time.

"Are you coming inside?" She was startled by the voice of a man walking toward her. She just stared at him. He was incredibly handsome with wide shoulders and a narrow waist. He was enough to take any woman's breath away. She imagined the feeling of having his hard, naked body pressed against hers. He interrupted her fantasy. She couldn't force an answer. "My name is Cliff. I don't recognize you. Is this your first time?"

Virginia nodded.

"We only use our first names. Once you're inside, you'll be surprised at just how quickly you get comfortable with everything. You're really going to like all the people in this group. They're all so friendly. I've been coming here for over three years." He extended his hand to Virginia. "Come with me. I'll stay with you and show you the ropes. Just remember, you don't have to do anything you don't want to do."

Virginia took his hand. They walked into the room and he led her to a sofa in the back of the room. A young woman was speaking. Virginia assumed she was explaining the rules for participation. Several other people spoke. After she'd heard the others talk, she knew intuitively that she had made the right decision. Cliff stood and went to the front of the room. He spoke for a few minutes in graphic detail about his many sexual escapades. All those gathered applauded when he'd finished, just as they'd applauded each speaker. When he returned to where Virginia was sitting, he leaned over and whispered, "Would you like to tell us about yourself now?"

Virginia gave him a slight nod. She whispered, "Yes, I think I need to, but I'm really nervous."

Once again Cliff extended his hand to her and smiled, "I'll go with you."

She took his hand. He led her to the front of the room. Excitement was streaming through her body. She looked out at the dozen or so people sitting patiently in the room. There were looks of empathy and understanding on every one of their faces. Then, in a shaking voice, Virginia repeated the sentence that she'd heard each of the speakers before her use. "Hello, my name is Virginia, and I'm a sex addict."

Chapter 40

"No, Almeda, this time I'm picking up the check. Sometimes you just need to let a friend do something for you."

Almeda nodded reluctantly and patted Steele on his hand. "You really are a dear, dear man. We count ourselves so lucky to have you as a friend." She took Horace's hand with her other. A tear rolled down her cheek.

Steele had invited Almeda and Horace to join him for lunch at a little café off Palm Street. It was actually a bakery. In addition to all the usual cookies, cakes, pies and various types of fresh baked bread, they also sold specialty sandwiches for lunch. There were only four small tables inside the bakery. There was a single umbrella-table that would seat four people on the side patio. Steele had called ahead and asked the owner to reserve the outside table for him. He wanted the privacy to talk with Horace and Almeda.

"This has got to be a major disappointment for both of you."

"I'd be less than truthful with you if I didn't admit it." Horace shrugged his shoulders. "I did the very thing that I said I was not going to do. I got caught up in it all. It's so seductive. I actually started thinking about my service of consecration and the folks I wanted to participate. I got excited about the idea of being a Bishop." Horace chuckled. "Hell, I even held a couple of purple shirts up in front of me at the department store just to see what I'd look like in purple. And if you'll excuse my vanity, I thought I looked pretty damned good."

"You look handsome in purple, Horace. You can still wear purple dress shirts whenever you want." Almeda squeezed his hand and forced herself to smile.

"Truth be told, I think this wonderful woman I'm married to is bearing the brunt of the disappointment. I think there's some truth to the adage that it's easier to suffer yourself than to see someone you love suffer." He leaned over and kissed her on the cheek.

"Have you given any more thought to fighting it?" Steele took another sip from his glass of sweet tea. "Everyone is talking about what Elmer Idle did. The word is getting around the Diocese. Bishop Peterson has offered to write a letter to all the Standing Committees. They can block this election by refusing to confirm Sean Evans."

"I know that, Steele. And believe me, there is a part of me that wants to fight back. I'm not so sure we couldn't win. But let's face it. We clergy just aren't very good street fighters. Think about what such a public fight would do to our Diocese and the larger Church. Almost half the clergy and laity weren't voting for me anyway. The Diocese is already divided. Sean only has the support of fifty percent of the folks right now."

"But you would have won had Elmer not been so devious."

"I think you're probably right about that, but think about what the press would do with it. A story like this will just put the Episcopal Church in an even worse light than some hold us in now. And what about First Church? I just don't want the newspapers to start running stories on how one of our own members has done in their own priest. And don't forget the potential of turning the entire mess into a race issue. No good can come from any of that, Steele."

Steele looked at Almeda. "And you feel the same way?"

"Tell him about the telephone call you received, Horace."

"Oh, I almost forgot. Steele, do you know an Earl Lafitte?"

Steele wrinkled his brow. "That name does sound familiar. I just can't place it."

"Well, he knows you. He doesn't have anything but wonderful things to say about you. He sang your praises for a good ten minutes. He's completely behind everything you've done here in Falls City. He was especially appreciative of the outreach work that we've been doing. He asked questions about each of our projects. He was particularly interested in Duke's House and Noah's House. He thinks you're a mighty brave man to have started those ministries for the gay folk in Falls City."

"Earl Lafitte. Earl Lafitte." Steele muttered over and over again. "I still can't place him, but the name is so familiar. Does he live here?"

"No, actually he's from the Diocese of San Francisco. He's President of the Standing Committee out there. He wants to fight this election and assures me that their Standing Committee will vote against Sean's election if I just give him the word."

Steele sat silent, trying to remember where he might have met the man. Then in the recesses of his mind a light went on. He smiled in recognition. He now understood. He remembered who Earl Lafitte was and who he must be now. He also knew exactly how Chadsworth was able to do what he'd done.

"What are you smiling about, Steele? Do you know this guy?"

Steele's smiled broadened. "I do now."

"As I was saying, Almeda and I have talked about it. For all the reasons we mentioned above, we're not going to challenge this election. I'm not going to put our parish, our Diocese, or the Episcopal Church through it. More than that—I'm not going to put Almeda through it. She's the light of my life. Our life together is not contingent on me being a bishop. In fact, our life will most likely be a lot less stressful and a lot happier if I just keep on doing what I'm doing right now."

Steele handed his credit card to the waiter that had been refilling their tea glasses. "I can't say I blame you. I'm disappointed for you and I'm disappointed for our Diocese. You are head and shoulders more qualified to be a Bishop than Sean Evans. Our Diocese and the Church have lost a wonderful opportunity to be led by you."

"Thanks for saying that. Of course, you know that you're prejudiced, but in a good way. We clergy are lovers. We're not fighters. It's in our DNA to be givers. That's why we do what we do. Above all, we're not going to sacrifice the Church and the people that we love over some turf war."

Steele nodded. "I know that you're right and I don't disagree, but I'm growing weary of being the one that always compromises or gives in. I'm tired of not fighting back. Sooner or later one of us needs to stand up to the politics that destroy so many of our brothers and sisters."

"That may be true, but it needs to be a battle worth winning. This battle is simply not worth fighting. What are you going to do with Elmer Idle?"

"I talked to Bishop Peterson about ex-communicating him, but he advised against it. He said that Sean would just reverse it when he becomes the Bishop. His counsel is to let the people in the parish and Diocese deal with him. His hunch is that they'll freeze him out. If enough folks give him the cold shoulder, he'll move on to another parish. The Bishop said we should let the Presbyterians have him."

Almeda gave Steele a determined look. "You can bet that everyone I know will turn their backs on him. His dirty tricks just can't continue. And as for that holier than thou wife of his, I've had enough of her as well."

Horace put his arm around her. "I understand your anger, but we're not going to let them turn us into bitter people. We're going to smile and move on with our lives."

"I hope you aren't asking me to be nice to them."

"No, I'm just saying that we're not going to become like them."

Steele stood and shook Horace's hand. "The good news is we get to continue to work together." He kissed Almeda on the cheek. "And I get to keep you as one of my closest friends in this parish."

"But we need to fight back. We've got to fight back."

Steele smiled. "And we will. Horace is right. It has to be the right battle and it has to be at the right time. We'll all know when the time is right."

Chapter 41

"FATHER AUSTIN, HERE'S the bottom line. Your wife was set up." It was the voice of Tim Roberts, the private detective that he'd hired.

Relief washed over Steele. It was as though the entire world had just decided to quit sitting on top of him. "Are you sure?"

"This is what my girl was able to find out. Someone hired him to pose for suggestive pictures with your wife. Your wife knew nothing about it. He took her by surprise and pretty much manipulated her into the various poses for the camera. She actually threatened to call security and have him removed from your club."

"My club?"

The detective chuckled. "Yea, the photos were taken at your neighborhood club by the pool. Your wife was there with another woman. They were tanning. The guy that paid him took him there."

"Does he know who paid him?"

"He wouldn't give us the guys name. He paid him in cash."

"Did you get a description?"

"He volunteered that he was a tall bag of bones. He was making fun of the guy. He said he was wearing an old suit that went out of style fifty years ago. He said he had an Adams Apple that kept dancing on the top of his bowtie. Do you have any idea as to who that might have been?"

Steele breathed a sigh of relief. "I know exactly who it was. In fact, there's not a single doubt in my mind."

"What do you plan to do?"

"I'm not sure just yet, but I want to thank you for getting to the bottom of all this. I honestly believe you've saved my marriage and my family. Thanks for clearing all this up for me."

"I'm glad to hear that. I fear that ninety-nine percent of the time, my investigations lead to the opposite result. It feels awfully nice to be the guy wearing the white hat for a change."

Steele turned his chair to look out his window. Evening was falling over the First Church cemetery. He watched the shadows play off the monuments. He was so relieved to know that Randi had been true to him. He so wanted to just rush home and hold her in his arms, but the monthly meeting of the Vestry was to begin in less than thirty minutes. He knew that he'd held her at a distance the last few weeks. He did it out of self-defense. The pictures had placed suspicion in his mind. He just couldn't open himself to her until he knew. He just couldn't be vulnerable with her. He didn't want her to be able to hurt him any further. Now he knew, but even with that knowledge, he felt so empty. He felt like a burned out house. He was sitting inside his own body staring out of empty windows. He was so tired.

"I understand you've had an investigator asking some questions about me?"

Steele turned in his chair toward the voice. His heart jumped into his throat. Anger rushed through him. He stood and stared at Ned Boone.

"What you have tried to do to me and my family is absolutely unforgivable!" Steele shouted.

Ned Boone walked confidently to Steele's desk and sat down in the visitor's chair. He smirked at Steele. "Well, I hope I've finally been able to get through to you."

Steele remained standing. "I don't remember asking you to be seated."

Ned grinned at him. "Here in the South, we always ask a gentleman to be seated."

"Sir, you are no gentleman." Steele was trying to control his anger. It was all he could do to keep from throwing himself across the desk and strangling Ned Boone with his bare hands.

"You're entitled to your opinion. Now are you going to resign or do I have to take those pictures to the next phase of my plan?"

"Those pictures are a scam."

"The people of this Church won't know that."

Steele wrinkled his brow. "What do the members of this church have to do with those pictures?"

Ned Boone stood. "You have a Vestry meeting in ten minutes. I suggest that you go in there and resign. If you fail to do so, I will have copies of those pictures in the mailbox of every member of this parish within twenty-four hours."

"And I'll send out a letter that will include my detective's report on just how they were taken and I will name you as the blackmailer."

"Such an ugly word, blackmail." Ned chuckled. "Misturh Austin, you're forgetting human nature. You might try to explain them, but most people are going to see through it. They're going to assume that where there's smoke there's fire. Your wife will become fodder for the town gossips. Neither of you will ever completely recover. So I suggest that you sit down and write out your letter of resignation. You just have a few minutes left before the Vestry meeting begins."

Steele was furious. "You mail out those pictures and I'll sue you for slander."

Ned Boone began laughing. "It'll be tossed out. You're a public figure. The people in this parish can say anything we want to say about you and there's absolutely nothing you can do about it."

"I've got at least a half dozen lawyers in this very parish that would love to test that statement in a court of law."

"I can say anything I want to about you or your wife and it doesn't even have to be true." With those words Steele lost it. He literally began running around the desk toward Ned. "And just what do you think you're doing?"

Steele grabbed Ned by the arm with one hand and the back of his pants by the other. He began to physically push Ned toward his office door. "I'm going to physically remove you from my office."

"Get your hands off me!" Steele began pushing Ned toward the door. "You're hurting me! You're going to be sorry."

When Steele got him to the door, he pushed him into the hallway and slammed the door to his office.

Chapter 42

THE VESTRY MEETING had already started when Steele walked into the conference room. Elmer Idle had taken it upon himself to preside. "Father Austin, we weren't sure you were going to make it, so I called the meeting to order. We have a full agenda."

Steele knew his face was still flushed. He waved his hand at Elmer. "Please, go on. Continue to preside." Steele sank down in the chair appointed for the Rector. Stone slid him a note. *What's going on with you?*

Steele just looked at him and shook his head. Stone slid him a second note. *I'm going to ask for a recess so we can talk.* Steele shook his head.

Elmer continued. "I hate to be the one to bring this up, but my telephone has been ringing off the hook. Father Austin, the people of this parish are just not happy about you turning our parish hall into a gambling casino."

Steele didn't even answer him. He just gave him a blank stare.

"That was a fundraiser put on by members of the American Legion." Chief Sparks spoke calmly. "The money raised went to a very good cause. I attended the event myself. Everything was in order. It was a wonderful evening and gave our parish some very positive press among the military veterans and their families. I see no reason to object to it."

"Well, the people in this parish have and do object to it." Elmer countered. "I need to know. Father Austin, do you ever plan to turn our parish into a gambling casino and saloon again?"

Once again, Steele just looked at Elmer. He couldn't even find the strength to give him an answer.

Stone ruled. "The Canons of the Church give the Rector complete discretion over the use of parish property. He was within his rights to loan the parish hall to the ladies of the American Legion. I suggest we move on to the next item on the agenda."

Elmer continued. "Well, that may be, but I want the minutes to reflect that I've registered the objections of the people in this parish. Now I need to let this Vestry know that a considerable number of our people have not accepted a woman priest in our parish. I have a petition signed by well over one hundred people asking that she not be allowed to preside at services. She can read the Gospel and distribute communion, but we do not want her pretending to celebrate the Eucharist. I am handing this petition directly to you, Father Austin. You hired her. Now you need to schedule her according to the desires of the members of this parish."

Elmer handed Steele the petition. Steele didn't even look at it. He simply handed it back to him without making any comment.

Elmer shrugged. "I once again want the minutes to reflect that I've recorded the objections of the people of this congregation. Now, Gary, what is this item you've placed on the agenda? You want to present a resolution for the separation of the school. We've already considered that once and rejected it."

Gary nodded. "I know that, but I along with several other members of the Vestry, believe the time has come for the parish to relinquish control over the school."

Elmer, Stone, the Chief and a couple of other members of the Vestry immediately registered angry objections to his statement. Elmer looked at Steele, "You agree with us, don't you, Father Austin?"

Steele looked at him. Then he looked at each member of the Vestry. They were all staring at him with questioning looks. Steele learned back in his chair. Silence hung in the room. "Gentlemen, I'm tired. I'm tired of arguing about the school and fundraisers, and outreach projects, the cemetery and all the rest. I'm exhausted. It's not the kind of exhaustion that a few days off will fix. I'm burned out and I now know it." Steele stood and started walking toward the conference room door. He opened it. "Guys, I'm adding one final thing to the agenda for you to consider and I want your answer tonight. You can either give me a sabbatical or you can put together a search committee to look for a new Rector. And men, I really don't care which one you choose. In the words of Rhett Butler—*frankly I don't give a damn*. Steele closed the door behind him and walked to his car. He didn't recall the drive home. He only knew that for the first time in years he felt free. He looked at his speedometer. He needed to slow down. He was forty miles over the speed limit. He just felt like he couldn't get away from First Church fast enough.

Chapter 43

STEELE OPENED THE door quietly. He didn't want to wake his children. He knew they would be sleeping. He went into the kitchen. Randi had wrapped his dinner plate with tin foil and left it for him on the counter. She'd also left him a note. It read simply, *Steele. We need to talk. I've made a decision.* He folded the note and climbed the stairs to their bedroom. Randi was sleeping. He walked across the hall to the nursery. Amanda had turned herself in the bed until her feet were hanging out through the crib bars. He gently lifted her and placed her back in the bed. She didn't even stir. She was sleeping so soundly. He walked down the hall to Travis' room. Travis, as was his nightly practice, had kicked his blanket off and it was lying on the floor. Steele picked it up and covered Travis with it. He kissed him on the forehead.

Back downstairs, Steele stretched out on the couch. He was just about to close his eyes when the telephone rang. He picked it up on the second ring. "Father, this is Stone."

"Yes, Stone."

"Father, the Vestry is very concerned about you. We have voted that you take a sabbatical, and the sooner the better."

"How about starting tomorrow morning?"

"I think that will be perfectly agreeable."

"Will six months be long enough?"

"I can only hope it is." Steele was silent. He was so tired.

"Hello? Are you still there?"

"Stone, was it unanimous?"

"No."

"I'm sorry to hear that."

"It doesn't matter. Those of us who love you want you to take care of yourself. Father, I love you."

"And I love you, Stone."

"Keep in touch while you're gone. Let me know what you're up to. Come back to us rested."

"Thanks, Stone."

With that, Steele hung up the phone and lay back down on the couch. "Who was that on the telephone?" Randi was sitting on the edge of the couch.

"Stone." Steele sat up so he could look at her. She was wearing a silk robe and he knew she had her silk shorty pajamas on under it. He wanted to grab her and just squeeze her. He wanted to tell her just how much he loved her.

"Steele, we have to talk."

"I know."

"I don't know what is going on with you, but I've decided I need a break. I want to take the children and go stay with my parents for awhile."

Steele took her hand in his. "I need to tell you some things. The first thing I need to tell you is that I just walked out of a Vestry meeting tonight. I told them that they could either give me a sabbatical or they could organize a search committee and look for a new Rector."

"Steele, you quit your job?"

"No, the reason that Stone called me was to let me know that they've voted to give me a six month sabbatical."

"God only knows how much you need it." Randi removed her hand from Steele's. "Do you love me?"

He recaptured her hand in his. "Honey, believe me, I know that I've not been acting like it, but if you'll let me, I'll do everything in my power to show you just how much I do love you. I'm going to devote this entire sabbatical to you and the children. I'm not going to give First Church a single thought."

He pulled Randi to him. He put his arms around her and kissed her. It was a long, slow, deep kiss. She put her arms around his neck. He could feel the tears running down her cheeks against his. When he released her, he wiped her tears with his hand. "I thought I'd done something to make you stop loving me."

"Randi, you've done nothing but be the perfect wife, mother and best friend any man could ever ask for. I'm so sorry for not treating you better. I've got a lot to tell you. We have so much to talk about, but not tonight."

"Why? Steele. Why? What's been going on with you?"

"For tonight, can I just focus on loving you? In time, I'll tell you all the things that have been bothering me, but believe me, Randi. You did nothing wrong. Absolutely nothing."

"Are they things about me?"

"No. No. A thousand times no. As far as I'm concerned, you're perfect."

Randi sat quietly looking at him. "Steele, have you thought about being something other than a priest?"

"I've thought about it. But Honey, I love being a priest. I love what I do. It gives me joy to be able to help people through their difficulties. I like celebrating the happy times with them. I want to be able to tell the Gospel story over and over again. It really is the greatest story that can ever be told. Randi, when I get to baptize a baby, it's one of the happiest moments of my life. Think about it. I am marking a child as Christ's very own forever. Or to preside at the marriage of a couple who, in this great big world, have not only managed to find each other, but to fall in love. And Randi, I know that you couldn't come to the Easter Service on Saturday, but Honey, there's just something about being in the congregation of the faithful hearing the scriptures read, joining them in prayer, and singing the hymns of praise to God. It's just what I've been put on this earth to do. I know that beyond a shadow of a doubt."

Randi nodded. "I know. Your eyes light up when you talk about your ministry. And you're really good at it." Randi bit her lower lip for a second as though she was trying to decide whether or not to say more. "But, Steele, some of them are so mean to you."

He nodded. "But the majority of them are wonderful. Ninety-nine percent of our congregation are faithful men and women trying to do the best they know how to do. They love their Lord and they love

His Church. They come to worship faithfully. They say their prayers and spend their days living lives of love and compassion. Those are the ones that we need to focus on. The Ned Boones of this world are always going to be with us. They are in the minority. They really don't represent the Church. I don't know if they're beyond redemption or not. I just know that I can't let them destroy me or the parish that God has given into my care."

"Steele, I just don't know how you do it. Some of the things that some of those people have done to you are just awful. It's as though attacking you is their full time job. How can you keep from hating them?"

"A very wise woman once said to me that *resentment is like drinking a cup of poison hoping the other person would die.* I prefer to simply pray for them and if truth be told, I feel sorry for them. Can you even imagine the kind of snakes that must crawl around in their heads?"

"Well, I need to tell you that I'm not there. I hate them for everything they've done to you and what they do to us. I really wish you'd move us away from here."

"I promise you that over the next six months we'll talk about doing that very thing. But Randi, my hunch is that there's a Ned Boone and an Elmer Idle in every parish in Christendom. "

"If that's true, then they need to be exposed for the evil work that they do."

"That's part of the problem. Evil often hides behind the mask of good. I think they've deceived themselves into thinking that by attacking me, they really are doing what is best for the parish. I'm convinced they're able to persuade far too many people that they're the guys in the white hats. My other fear is that they really don't care how many people they hurt in the process of getting their own way. I don't think they care if it chases people away from the Church. My hunch is that's what they want. They'd rather be big fish in a smaller pond."

"But their deeds are done in darkness. They're the worst kind of liars. They distort the truth and then present it as the Gospel."

"I know. But as of this minute I am on sabbatical. We don't have to think about the Ned Boones of this world for at least six months. So let's forget them and just focus on healing the damage they have been able to do to both of us and our marriage."

She breathed a sigh of relief. "What are we going to do first?"

"Would you mind if I went with you and the children to stay with your parents for awhile?"

Randi threw her arms around Steele's neck. "It's so nice to have you back. I love you so much."

"And I love you."

Steele picked her up in his arms and carried her up the stairs to their bedroom. He made slow tender love to his wife that night. Their souls once again found each other and were united. Then he held her in his arms as they slept. He slept a restful, undisturbed sleep. The sweet smell of the magnolia tree outside the open window filled their room.

Epilogue

ON THE FIRST morning of his sabbatical, Steele stopped at his office to advise the staff that he would be gone for six months. During his absence, Horace would be in charge of the parish. He met with Crystal to give her instructions on what to do with his mail and various telephone calls. He was just about to leave when a special delivery envelope arrived for him. He took it into his office and opened it. Inside were the three pictures of Randi and the male model. Only this time the photos had been doctored. Someone had reworked them so as to remove the top of Randi's bikini. They made her appear as though she were standing bare-breasted with the man. A note was attached to the last photo.

Mister Austin, I understand that you are going on sabbatical. **DO NOT RETURN TO FIRST CHURCH!** *If you do, these are the photos that will be in every mailbox in Falls City before your car enters the city limits.*

Steele pushed the intercom button to Crystal's office.

"Yes, Father Austin. I thought you'd left."

"No, I'm still here. I want you to get Stone Clemons and Henry Mudd on the telephone for me. Link us all together. I want it to be a conference call."

"When?"

"Do it now if that is at all possible."

Steele sat down in his chair and turned to look out at the First Church steeple. The sky was so blue and there were just a few white clouds hanging in the sky. The cemetery surrounding the church looked so peaceful and serene. The lawn was gracefully splattered with wild-flowers of all colors. The white blossoms on the magnolia trees glistened against their dark green leaves. In spite of the picture painted outside his window, he now knew that someone needed to fight. He was that someone. This time he'd fight Ned Boone and all those like him. He'd do it for himself and for Randi. But he'd also do it for all the clergy who have been sabotaged by wolves dressed in sheep's clothing. He resolved not to do it on their turf. He won't do it in the gutter. He will fight them in a Court of Law. He will challenge Ned's assertion that clergy are public figures and therefore open targets for slander and innuendo. He intended to prove that under the law of this land, people cannot say anything they want about their priests or their families and get away with it.

Steele continued to look at the peaceful portrait both God and man and painted outside his office window. A smile spread over his face. He was no longer angry. He was at peace with his decision. He knew it was the right one to make. He uttered out loud. "It's the right battle. It's the right time. This has to be done."

ABOUT THE AUTHOR

THE REVEREND DOCTOR Dennis R. Maynard is the author of nine books. Well over 100,000 Episcopalians have read his book, *Those Episkopols*. 2500 congregations around the United States use *Those Episkopols* in their new member ministries. Several denominational leaders have called it the unofficial handbook for the Episcopal Church. He is also the author of *Forgive and Get Your Life Back*, which has been used by the same number of clergy to do forgiveness training in their congregations

His most recent endeavors are earning him a reputation as a novelist. The books in *The Magnolia Series* are growing in popularity around the nation as readers anxiously await each new chapter.

"The novels give us a chance to look at the underside of parish life. While the story lines are fictional, the readers invariably think they recognize the characters. If not, they know someone just like the folks that attend First Episcopal Church in the town of Falls City, Georgia."

Over his thirty-eight years of parish ministry he has served some of the largest congregations in the Episcopal Church. His ministry included parishes in Illinois, Oklahoma, South Carolina, Texas, and California. President George H.W. Bush and his family are members of the congregation he served in Houston, Texas. It is also the largest parish in the Episcopal Church.

He has served other notable leaders that represent the diversity of his ministry. These national leaders include Former Secretary of State, James Baker; Former Secretary of Education, Richard Riley; Supreme Court Nominee, Clement Haynsworth; and the infamous baby doctor, Benjamin Spock, among others.

Doctor Maynard maintains an extensive speaking and travel schedule. He is frequently called on to speak, lead retreats, or serve as a consultant to parishes, schools, dioceses, and organizations throughout the United States.

Maynard earned an Associate of Arts Degree in psychology, a Bachelor of Arts Degree in the social sciences, a Masters Degree in theology, and a Doctor of Ministry Degree. He currently resides in Rancho Mirage, California with his wife, Nancy, *and their daughter's cat,* Lila.

To invite Dr. Maynard to speak at your parish or organization, please visit his web site www.Episkopols.com or email him at Episkopols@aol.com.

Made in the USA